THE MISSING YEARS

THE REAL STORY OF JESUS BEYOND THE GOSPELS

UNIVERSE MAKER FROM NAZARETH
BOOK ONE

MICHAEL VINCENT

HAVONA PRESS

CONTENTS

INTRODUCTION

Everyone knows Jesus. Or thinks they do.

The carpenter from Nazareth. The itinerant preacher. The miracle worker. The man crucified on a Roman cross. The founder—or at least the inspiration—for the world's largest religion. Two billion people call themselves Christians. Countless more respect him as a prophet, a teacher, a moral exemplar. His teachings have shaped Western civilization. His life has been painted, sculpted, filmed, debated, worshipped, and analyzed for two thousand years.

Yet for all this familiarity, the Jesus most people know is strangely incomplete. The Gospel accounts, for all their power and influence, provide only fragments of a life. A birth narrative, a single childhood episode at age twelve, then silence until he emerges at approximately thirty years of age to begin his public ministry. Three years of teaching compressed into selective episodes. A trial, a crucifixion, a resurrection, an ascension—and then the story ends.

What happened during those first thirty years? How did a carpenter's son from an obscure Galilean village develop such profound wisdom that his words still challenge humanity two millennia later? What experiences shaped him? What trials did he face? How did he come to understand his own identity and mission? The traditional sources offer very little.

This book series presents the complete life of Jesus of Nazareth.

It draws upon sources that provide what the Gospel writers could not —a detailed, year-by-year account of the child, the adolescent, the young man, and finally the teacher whose brief public ministry would reshape human history. Here you will find the Jesus who spent over fifteen years as a working carpenter supporting his widowed mother and seven younger siblings. The Jesus who traveled throughout the Mediterranean world, learning how humanity lived and thought across diverse cultures. The Jesus who genuinely struggled with the weight of his mission, who experienced authentic human emotions, who grew in wisdom through the same processes of learning and experience that shape every human life.

The narrative that follows is not speculative fiction or imaginative reconstruction. Every detail rests upon source material that will be fully disclosed in this this book. Readers may initially wonder how such comprehensive biographical information could exist for a figure whose life predates modern historical methods by two thousand years. That question will be answered after the story itself has been told. The author asks only that readers engage with the narrative on its own terms, evaluating the account by its internal coherence, its psychological authenticity, and its explanatory power, before turning to questions of sourcing.

What emerges from this account is a Jesus both more human and more extraordinary than conventional portraits have allowed. More human because we see him not as a divine figure moving serenely through a predetermined script, but as a genuine person navigating genuine challenges—family obligations, economic pressures, religious controversies, political dangers, and the profound inner struggle of understanding who he was and what he had come to do. More extraordinary because the scope of his teaching, the consistency of his character, and the nature of his mission exceed anything that conventional accounts have conveyed.

The birth narrative alone reveals how much has been lost or distorted in transmission. The familiar Christmas story—the inn with no room, the stable, the shepherds and their angelic announcement, the wise men following a star—bears only partial resemblance to what actually occurred. Some elements are accurate. Others are legendary additions that accrued over decades of oral transmission before the Gospels were written. Still others are misunderstandings that arose when Gentile writers, unfamiliar with Jewish customs and Palestinian geography, recorded traditions they did not fully comprehend.

The account presented here corrects these distortions while honoring what the Gospel writers got right. It fills the vast silences with detailed narrative. It provides context that makes sense of episodes that have puzzled readers for centuries. And ultimately, it reveals dimensions of Jesus's identity that will challenge everything readers thought they knew about who he was and why his life mattered.

But that revelation must be earned through engagement with the story itself. The reader who skips ahead seeking quick answers will miss the very foundation that makes those answers meaningful. The life must be encountered before its significance can be grasped. The man must be known before his nature can be understood.

What follows, then, is a biography. It begins where all human lives begin—with parents, with circumstances, with a birth in a specific place at a specific time. It proceeds through childhood and adolescence, through young adulthood and the assumption of family responsibilities, through years of travel and preparation, and finally into the public ministry that would end on a Roman cross and continue beyond the grave.

It is the story of Joshua ben Joseph, known to history as Jesus of Nazareth—rendered here in fuller detail than any previous account has provided.

The man everyone thinks they know is about to become someone most have never truly met.

THE ROAD TO BETHLEHEM

IN MARCH OF 8 B.C., CAESAR AUGUSTUS ISSUED A DECREE THAT WOULD set in motion a chain of events culminating in history's most significant birth. The emperor ordered that all inhabitants of the Roman Empire should be numbered, a census intended to improve the efficiency of imperial taxation. This administrative directive, routine from Rome's perspective, created massive disruption throughout the provinces as families were required to return to their ancestral cities for registration. The Jews had always harbored deep cultural prejudice against any attempt to enumerate their people. This resistance, rooted in ancient tradition and reinforced by their sense of religious distinctiveness, combined with the serious domestic difficulties then plaguing Herod, King of Judea, to delay implementation of the census in the Palestinian kingdom. While the rest of the Roman Empire completed its registration in 8 B.C., the Jewish territories would not conduct their census until the following year. It was this postponement that determined the timing of events to come.

Joseph, a carpenter from the Galilean village of Nazareth, found himself subject to this decree in the summer of 7 B.C. His wife Mary was approaching the final weeks of pregnancy, yet the machinery of empire made no accommodation for personal circumstances. As a descendant of the house of David—though through adoption rather than direct lineage, his paternal ancestor six generations back having been an orphan taken in by one Zadoc, a direct descendant of David—Joseph was required to register in Bethlehem, the ancestral City of David, some ninety miles south of Nazareth.

There was no legal requirement for Mary to accompany her husband on this journey. Joseph was fully authorized to register for his entire family, and given her advanced condition, prudence suggested she remain in Nazareth. But Mary was an adventurous and determined woman, and she insisted on making the trip. She feared being left alone should the child arrive while Joseph was away. Moreover, Bethlehem lay not far from the City of Judah, where her kinswoman Elizabeth resided with Zacharias and their infant son John, born just five months earlier. The prospect of visiting Elizabeth, who had done so much to strengthen Mary's faith during her own pregnancy, added to her resolve.

Joseph initially forbade his wife from making the journey. His objections were practical and heartfelt—the distance was considerable, the terrain difficult, and Mary was heavy with child. But his protests proved futile. When Joseph discovered that Mary had already packed double rations of food for the trip, he recognized that further resistance was pointless. By the time they departed from their humble Nazareth home in the early morning hours of August 18, 7 B.C., Joseph had fully reconciled himself to his wife's decision, and they set forth together in good spirits.

The young couple's circumstances were modest. The building and furnishing of their home had been a significant financial burden, and Joseph was also contributing to the support of his parents, his father having recently become disabled. They possessed only a single beast of burden, and their savings had been largely depleted. Mary, being large with child, rode upon the donkey with their provisions, while Joseph walked alongside, leading the animal by its halter. They would travel this way for the entire journey—the young wife riding, the carpenter husband walking—through the late summer heat of the Palestinian lowlands.

The most direct route from Nazareth to Bethlehem would have passed through Samaria, following the central ridge road through Jacob's well and Bethel. Joseph and his family would have preferred this path. But the Jews of that era harbored deep antipathy toward the Samaritans and avoided contact with them whenever possible. Rather than risk the social and religious contamination that such passage might entail, the Nazareth couple chose the longer eastern route, turning at Jezreel to skirt around Mount Gilboa and descend into the Jordan valley.

Their first day of travel carried them southward around the foothills of Mount Gilboa. As they journeyed, they passed the ancient village of Shunem, and Joseph recounted to Mary the stories associated with that place—a woman said to be the most beautiful in Israel, and the miracles Elisha had worked in that very place. Passing by Jezreel, they spoke of the treachery of Ahab and Jezebel, and how Jehu had avenged their crimes. As they rounded Mount Gilboa itself, Joseph told the story of Saul, who had taken his own life on these very slopes, and of King David and the history embedded in these hills. The landscape itself was a testament to their people's long and turbulent history.

By evening they had descended to the banks of the Jordan River, where they made camp for the night beneath the stars. As they rested, Joseph and Mary fell into conversation about the child soon to be born and what manner of son he would become. Joseph continued to hold a more spiritual conception of their child's future mission, envisioning him as a great teacher who would enlighten his people. Mary, influenced by her family's prominent connection to the Maccabean tradition, still inclined toward the expectation of a Jewish Messiah—a political deliverer who would restore the fortunes of the Hebrew nation and free them from foreign domination. These differing perspectives would persist throughout their lives together, though both parents shared an unshakeable conviction that their firstborn was destined for some extraordinary purpose.

<hr>

Early on the morning of August 19, the couple resumed their journey southward through the Jordan valley. The road descended into increasingly tropical terrain as they traveled, and they laid aside their outer garments in the growing warmth. The landscape transformed around them into something almost paradisiacal—luxurious fields of grain stretched toward the horizon, and oleanders heavy with pink blossoms lined the way. The Jordan itself wound beside them, twisting endlessly, its waters glinting in the sunlight as they flowed southward toward the Dead Sea. To the north, massive Mount Hermon still dominated the skyline, its snow-capped peak glistening white in majestic splendor, almost three thousand feet of its upper slopes covered with perpetual snow—a striking contrast to the warmth of the valley below.

A little over three hours' travel from opposite Scythopolis, they came upon a bubbling spring, and here they paused. As they rounded the base of Gilboa, the travelers could see the Greek city of Scythopolis on their right, its marble structures gleaming in the distance. They gazed upon the magnificent buildings from afar but did not venture near the gentile city, to avoid any contact with its gentile population that might render them ritually unclean.

On their second day's journey, they passed by where the Jabbok flows from the east into the Jordan. Looking up this river valley, Joseph recounted the days of Gideon, when the Midianites had poured through this region to overrun the land. The ancient stories lived in every feature of the landscape.

Toward the end of the second day's travel, they made camp near the base of Mount Sartaba, the highest mountain overlooking the Jordan valley. Its summit was occupied by the Alexandrian fortress where

Herod had imprisoned one of his wives and buried two of his strangled sons—a grim reminder of the political dangers that lurked even in this time of relative peace.

The third day carried them past two villages recently built by Herod, and they noted the impressive stonework and lush palm groves that marked the king's construction projects. By nightfall they reached the ancient city of Jericho, where they stopped at an inn on the highway in the outskirts of the city to rest for the night. That evening, over their meal, the conversation among the travelers turned to familiar grievances—the oppressiveness of Roman rule, the heavy hand of Herod's taxation, the census enrollment that had displaced so many families, and the relative merits of Jerusalem and Alexandria as centers of Jewish learning and culture. After the evening discourse, the Nazareth travelers retired for the night's rest.

Early in the morning of August 20, they resumed their journey for the final day of travel. They now began to climb out of the Jordan valley, ascending the hills that led up to Jerusalem. As they neared the top of the ridge, they could look back across the Jordan to the mountains beyond, and south over the sluggish waters of the Dead Sea. About halfway up to Jerusalem, Joseph pointed ahead, and Mary caught her first glimpse of the Mount of Olives. Just beyond that ridge, Joseph told her, lay the Holy City itself. The young wife's heart quickened at the thought of soon beholding Jerusalem and the magnificent temple of their God.

On the eastern slopes of Olivet, they paused for rest in the borders of a small village called Bethany. Villagers emerged to offer assistance to the tired travelers, and Joseph and Mary stopped to rest near the home of a man named Simon, who had three children about the ages that their own child would soon reach—Mary, Martha, and Lazarus. The family invited the Nazareth travelers in for refreshment, and a friendship was formed that day that would endure for decades. Many times afterward, in the eventful years to come, Jesus would find welcome and rest in this very home.

They pressed on from Bethany, and soon stood on the brow of Olivet itself. There before them, spread across the opposite ridge, lay Jerusalem in all its magnificence. Mary beheld the Holy City, the imposing palaces, and most glorious of all, the inspiring temple of their God. The late morning sun illuminated the white marble and gilded ornamentation of the sanctuary. For a long moment they simply stood and gazed, taking in the sight that every devout Jew longed to see.

But they did not linger. It was now past midday on Thursday, and their destination still lay six miles further south. They descended the Mount of Olives, entered Jerusalem, and passed through the city. They paused briefly at the temple, and Mary was deeply moved by the throngs of worshippers assembled from every corner of the known world. But the urgency of reaching Bethlehem before Mary's condition worsened pressed them onward. They exited through the southern gate and followed the ancient road toward the City of David.

By midafternoon they reached Bethlehem. The small town had been transformed by the census into a scene of crowded chaos. As the ancestral home of David's lineage, it drew descendants from throughout the Jewish world, all seeking lodging simultaneously. The town's limited facilities—a handful of public inns and private homes willing to take in travelers—were completely overwhelmed.

The inn was overcrowded when Joseph inquired, and he was turned away. He then sought lodgings among his distant relatives in the town, for his family had ancestral connections to Bethlehem stretching back generations. But every household was already filled to capacity with visiting kinsmen who had returned for the enrollment. Every room in Bethlehem was occupied, every available space already claimed.

Joseph returned to the courtyard of the inn, uncertain what to do. Mary was exhausted from three days of travel and clearly distressed. Here the innkeeper offered an unexpected solution. The caravan stables beneath the inn, he explained, had been cleared of animals and cleaned up for the reception of the overflow of lodgers. These chambers had been hewn from the limestone rock, carved out of the hillside in the manner common to that region. One of these underground rooms had formerly served as a grain storage chamber, located at the front of the complex, before the stalls and mangers. Tent curtains had been hung to provide a measure of privacy.

Leaving the donkey in the courtyard, Joseph shouldered their bags of clothing and provisions and helped Mary descend the stone steps to their lodgings below. The room was dry and reasonably clean, the air cool after the heat of the day. Under the circumstances, they counted themselves fortunate to have found any shelter at all. Here, in this humble underground chamber beneath the inn of Bethlehem, in what had once been a grain storage room, they would await the birth of their child.

Joseph had intended to go out immediately to complete his census registration, but Mary was weary and considerably distressed. She asked him to stay with her, and he did.

The journey was complete. After three days of travel through the historic landscape of their ancestors, past mountains and rivers laden with the memories of their people, through the tropical beauty of the Jordan valley and up the Judean hills to Jerusalem and beyond, the young couple from Nazareth had reached their destination.

They could not know, as they settled into that rock-hewn chamber beneath the Bethlehem inn, that they had arrived at the appointed place at the appointed time. The child that Mary carried would be born within hours, in circumstances more humble than either parent had imagined. But in that humility lay a profound significance that would only become apparent in the fullness of time. The creator of a universe entered his own creation not in a palace or a temple, but in a converted storage room, among the common people, sharing from his first breath the ordinary circumstances of ordinary humanity.

The night descended over Bethlehem, and Mary rested as best she could while Joseph kept watch. All was quiet in the underground chamber. Above them, the crowded inn continued its bustle of displaced travelers. Somewhere in the town, Roman officials prepared for another day of census registration. In Jerusalem, Herod brooded in his palace. And in the stillness of that converted stable, a young wife waited for the birth pangs that would soon begin, unaware that she was about to bring into the world the child whose life would divide all of human history.[1]

2

THE BIRTH OF JOSHUA

That night Mary's condition worsened. She was restless and uncomfortable, unable to sleep for more than brief intervals. Joseph kept watch beside her as the hours passed, neither of them finding real rest. By the time the first gray light of dawn began to filter into their underground chamber, it was clear that the child would not wait much longer. The pangs of childbirth were unmistakable.

Throughout the morning hours, Mary labored in that rock-hewn room beneath the Bethlehem inn. Several women from among the traveling families lodging above came to assist her, providing the care that women have always provided one another in childbirth. Joseph waited anxiously, his prayers ascending constantly to the God of his fathers.

At noon on August 21, 7 B.C., Mary was delivered of a male child. The birth itself was utterly ordinary. In the same way that every baby before and since has entered the world, this child of promise began his human life. There were no supernatural signs, no celestial phenomena visible to human eyes. A young woman gave birth to her firstborn son in the most humble of circumstances, aided by strangers who showed kindness to a family far from home.

Mary took the infant in her arms. She had brought swaddling clothes from Nazareth, having prepared for the possibility that the child might come during their journey, and she wrapped the newborn carefully in these garments. Joseph prepared a place in a nearby manger, filling it with clean straw, and there they laid the baby to rest. The child was healthy and strong, crying vigorously as newborns do, showing no sign that anything distinguished this birth from countless others occurring across the world that same day.

They named him Joshua, in accordance with the instruction the celestial messenger had given to Mary nearly nine months before. The name meant "Yahweh is salvation," and it was common among the Jewish people, carrying echoes of the great hero who had led Israel into the promised land. In the Greek-speaking world into which this child would eventually carry his message, the name would be rendered as Jesus.

On the eighth day after his birth, in accordance with Jewish law and custom, the child was circumcised and formally given his name. Joseph and Mary had now fulfilled the first of the religious obligations incumbent upon the parents of a Jewish son.

The day following the birth, Joseph went into Bethlehem to complete his census registration. In the enrollment hall, he encountered a man he had spoken with two nights earlier at the inn in Jericho. This acquaintance introduced Joseph to a well-to-do friend who was lodging at the inn in proper quarters, and this man graciously offered to exchange accommodations with the young family from Nazareth. That afternoon, Joseph moved Mary and the infant up from the underground stable chamber to the inn itself, where they would have more suitable lodgings for the mother's recovery.

They remained at the inn for almost three weeks before finding more permanent accommodations in the home of a distant relative of Joseph. The family's plans had changed substantially since their arrival in Bethlehem. Both Joseph and Mary had become increasingly convinced, through their conversations with Zacharias and Elizabeth, that their son was destined to become the deliverer long promised to the Jewish people. The City of David seemed a more fitting place than remote Nazareth to raise one who might grow up to inherit the throne of Israel.

It was during these early weeks in Bethlehem that an unusual visit occurred. Three priests from the distant city of Ur in Mesopotamia arrived seeking the newborn child. These were not the wandering astrologers of later legend, nor did any star guide them to a manger. Rather, they had been informed by Zacharias, who maintained correspondence with religious teachers throughout the Jewish diaspora, that a child of great promise had been born.

These priests from Ur had been told by a strange religious teacher in their own country that he had experienced a dream in which he was informed that "the light of life" was about to appear on earth as a babe among the Jews. They had journeyed first to Jerusalem, spending many weeks in fruitless search, and were on the point of returning home when they encountered Zacharias. The aged priest disclosed his belief that Jesus was the object of their quest and directed them southward to Bethlehem.

The priests found the family in their lodgings and presented gifts to Mary for the child. Jesus was nearly three weeks old at the time of their visit—a healthy infant, growing as all babies grow, giving no outward sign of the extraordinary nature that would one day manifest in his life and teachings. The visitors from Ur paid their respects and departed, carrying back to Mesopotamia their account of what they had seen.

Later generations would embroider this simple visit with supernatural elements. The beautiful legend of the star of Bethlehem arose from an astronomical anomaly—on May 29 of that same year, an extraordinary conjunction of Jupiter and Saturn had occurred in the constellation of Pisces, and similar conjunctions followed on September 29 and December 5. These remarkable but entirely natural celestial events, occurring in the same year as the birth of Jesus, provided the basis for the well-meaning embellishments of later believers. People of that era delighted in such stories, and in an age when knowledge passed primarily by word of mouth, myths easily became traditions and traditions eventually came to be accepted as facts.

The Gospel narratives would later place shepherds at the scene of the birth, responding to angelic announcements in the fields outside Bethlehem. The truth was at once simpler and more profound. No human ears heard the celestial celebration that marked this birth. Angels did indeed gather to celebrate over the Bethlehem manger, but their songs of praise occurred on spiritual levels beyond human awareness. No shepherds came to pay homage on that first night, and no visitors arrived until the priests from Ur appeared weeks later.

The simple facts of the birth needed no embellishment to convey their significance. Here was a child born in the most ordinary way, under humble circumstances, to parents of modest means, in an occupied land under foreign rule. He entered the world not in a palace or a temple, but in an underground chamber used for storing grain, laid to rest in a feeding trough for animals. Everything about his birth proclaimed that this would be a life lived among the common people, sharing their experiences, understanding their struggles, accessible to all who sought truth regardless of their station.

Joseph and Mary remained in Bethlehem for over a year following the birth. Joseph found work in the town, practicing his trade as a carpenter, while Mary cared for the infant and later visited with Elizabeth, who traveled from the City of Judah with young John to see her kinswoman and the child of promise. The two mothers spoke often of their sons and the futures that had been announced to them, though neither could fully comprehend what lay ahead.

But dark clouds were gathering. Herod's spies had noted the visit of the priests from Ur, and word of their inquiries about a newborn "king of the Jews" had reached the king's suspicious ears. The aging monarch, who had already murdered members of his own family to protect his throne, would not ignore reports of a potential rival, even one still in infancy. The brief season of peace that the young family had enjoyed in Bethlehem was drawing to a close.

The child, meanwhile, grew as all children grow—sleeping and waking, nursing and crying, gradually becoming aware of the world around him. His eyes began to focus and follow movement. He learned to smile at familiar faces. He reached for objects and grasped his mother's finger. In every observable way, he was simply a baby, experiencing the universal stages of human infancy, dependent on his parents for every need.

Yet this same child, lying in a manger in Bethlehem, wrapped in common cloth, attended by ordinary people in an ordinary place, was destined to transform human understanding of God and eternity. The creator of a universe had entered his own creation, not in power and glory, but in weakness and obscurity. He had chosen to begin his human journey in circumstances that would be familiar to the vast majority of humanity—in poverty, in simplicity, among working people.

This was the birth of Joshua ben Joseph, whom the world would come to know as Jesus of Nazareth—a birth so ordinary in its outward circumstances, so extraordinary in its ultimate significance, that humanity has never ceased to contemplate its meaning. He came into the world as all humans come, helpless and dependent, and he would live among his fellow mortals as one of them, sharing their joys and sorrows, their hopes and uncertainties, until the hour came for him to reveal the full measure of truth he had come to bestow.[1]

3

THE EARLY YEARS

JEWISH LAW REQUIRED THAT EVERY FIRSTBORN SON BE PRESENTED AT THE temple in Jerusalem and redeemed through payment to the priests. Moses had taught that every firstborn belonged to the Lord, and instead of the sacrifice that had been customary among pagan peoples, such a son could be redeemed by paying five shekels to any authorized priest. A separate Mosaic ordinance directed that a mother, after a prescribed period following childbirth, should present herself at the temple for ritual purification, or have someone make the proper sacrifice on her behalf. It was customary to perform both ceremonies at the same time, and accordingly, several weeks after the birth, Joseph and Mary traveled up to Jerusalem with the infant to fulfill these obligations.

Their financial circumstances were evident in the offering they presented. The law permitted those of means to sacrifice a lamb for the mother's purification, but for families who could not afford this, two young pigeons were acceptable. Joseph deemed himself sufficiently poor to warrant this lesser offering. The small family made their way through the crowded temple courts, one young couple among many who came daily to fulfill the ancient requirements.

Two remarkable individuals frequented the temple courts in those days—Simeon, a singer from Judea, and Anna, a poetess from Galilee. Both were advanced in years, and both were close friends of the priest Zacharias, who had confided to them the secret of John and Jesus. Zacharias had shared his conviction that Jesus was the promised deliverer of the Jewish people, and both Simeon and Anna longed to see this child of destiny.

Zacharias knew the day Joseph and Mary were expected to appear at the temple, and he had prearranged with his two friends that he would indicate, by raising his hand in salute, which child in the procession of firstborns was Jesus. When the moment came, Anna had prepared a poem for the occasion, and Simeon sang it before the assembled worshippers in the temple courts, much to the astonishment of Joseph and Mary and all who had gathered. The hymn spoke of redemption and salvation, of light for the gentiles and glory for Israel, of ancient promises now fulfilled. The words were beautiful, but they carried implications that troubled the young parents.

On their way back to Bethlehem afterward, Joseph and Mary traveled in silence, confused and somewhat overwhelmed by what had occurred. Mary was particularly disturbed by the farewell words Anna had spoken to her, and Joseph found himself uncomfortable with this premature effort to identify Jesus as the expected Messiah of the Jewish people.

The family settled into life in Bethlehem following the temple presentation. Both Joseph and Mary had become convinced, largely through their conversations with Zacharias and Elizabeth, that their son was destined to become the Jewish deliverer, the Messiah long promised to their people. For more than a year the family remained in Bethlehem, little suspecting the danger that was gathering around them.

Herod's spies had not been idle. When they reported to the king that priests from Ur had visited Bethlehem seeking a newborn child, Herod summoned these Chaldeans to appear before him. He inquired diligently about the new "king of the Jews," but the visitors gave him little satisfaction, explaining only that the child had been born to a woman who had come to Bethlehem with her husband for the census enrollment. Herod, unsatisfied with this answer, sent them away with a purse of money and instructions to find the child so that he too might come and pay homage—since they had declared that the child's kingdom was to be spiritual rather than temporal. But the wise men did not return to Herod.

When they failed to reappear, the king grew suspicious. His informers soon brought him additional troubling news: reports of what had occurred at the temple during the redemption ceremonies, including portions of the hymn that Simeon had sung. But these same informers had failed to follow Joseph and Mary when they departed, and they could not tell Herod where the family had taken the child. The king was furious at this failure and dispatched searchers to locate them.

Knowing that Herod was pursuing the Nazareth family, Zacharias and Elizabeth remained away from Bethlehem during this dangerous period. The infant Jesus was secreted with Joseph's relatives while the search continued. Joseph was afraid to seek work openly, and their small savings rapidly dwindled. The young family lived in fear and uncertainty, never knowing when Herod's agents might discover them.

When, after more than a year of searching, Herod's spies had still not located Jesus, the king's patience finally broke. Suspecting that the child remained concealed somewhere in Bethlehem, he prepared a terrible order: a systematic search of every house in the town, and the execution of all male children under two years of age. In this manner, Herod calculated, the child who was to become "king of the Jews" would certainly be destroyed, whatever his hiding place.

The massacre occurred in mid-October of 6 B.C., when Jesus was a little over one year old. Sixteen infant boys perished in Bethlehem that day. But intrigue and murder, even within his own immediate family, were commonplace at Herod's court, and this atrocity attracted little notice beyond the grief-stricken families who suffered its horror.

There were, however, believers in the coming Messiah even among Herod's court attendants. One of these, learning of the order to slaughter the Bethlehem children, communicated the warning to Zacharias, who in turn dispatched a messenger to Joseph. The warning came barely in time. The night before the massacre, Joseph and Mary departed from Bethlehem with the infant, fleeing toward Egypt. They traveled alone to avoid attracting attention, making their way south and west toward Alexandria. Zacharias had provided funds for the journey, and the small family pressed on as quickly as Mary and the child could manage. Behind them, in Bethlehem, the terrible order was carried out. Before them lay exile in a foreign land.

Alexandria, the great Egyptian metropolis, was home to a substantial Jewish population and offered both safety and opportunity. Joseph secured work shortly after their arrival, initially employed as a carpenter and later elevated to the position of foreman over a large group of workmen constructing one of the city's public buildings. This new experience gave him the idea of eventually becoming a contractor and builder after they returned to Palestine.

The family lived with well-to-do relatives of Joseph who had settled in Alexandria, and they were able to establish a reasonably normal life. Mary maintained a constant vigil over the child during these early years of helpless infancy, fearful that anything might befall him that could jeopardize his welfare or interfere with his future mission. No mother was ever more devoted to her child.

In the home where they stayed there were two other children about Jesus's age, and among the near neighbors there were six others whose ages were sufficiently close to make them acceptable playmates. At first Mary was inclined to keep Jesus close by her side, fearing that something might happen to him if he were allowed to play in the garden with the other children. But Joseph, with the assistance of his kinsfolk, convinced her that such overprotection would deprive Jesus of the valuable experience of learning how to interact with children his own age. Mary came to realize that excessive sheltering might make the child self-conscious and self-centered, and she finally gave her assent to allowing him to grow up like any other child—though she made it her business to remain on watch whenever the little ones played about the house or in the garden.

Throughout the two years of their sojourn in Alexandria, Jesus enjoyed good health and continued to grow normally. Aside from a few close friends and relatives, no one was told that he was a child of special promise. One of Joseph's relatives did reveal this to a few friends in Memphis, descendants of the distant Ikhnaton, and these Egyptian believers, together with a small group from Alexandria, assembled at the home of Joseph's relative-benefactor shortly before the family's return to Palestine. They wished the Nazareth family well and paid their respects to the child they believed was destined for greatness. On this occasion, the assembled friends presented Jesus with a complete copy of the Greek translation of the Hebrew scriptures—the Septuagint—a gift of immense value that would profoundly influence his education in the years ahead.

These Alexandrian believers urged Joseph and Mary to remain in Egypt, insisting that the child of destiny would be able to exert far greater world influence as a resident of Alexandria than from any location in Palestine. Their persuasions delayed the family's departure for some time. But when news finally reached them that Herod had died, Joseph and Mary made ready to return to their homeland. They departed from Alexandria on a boat belonging to their friend Ezraeon, sailing for the port of Joppa and arriving late in August of 4 B.C.

From there they went directly to Bethlehem, where they spent the entire month of September in counsel with their friends and relatives, deliberating whether they should remain in Judea or return to Nazareth. Mary had never fully abandoned the idea that Jesus ought to grow up in Bethlehem, the City of David. She believed it the most appropriate place for the new candidate for David's throne to be reared. Joseph, however, harbored serious doubts. He knew that he himself was not truly a descendant of David—that his connection to the royal line came only through the adoption of an ancestor six generations back. More practically, he feared for the child's safety in Judea. Herod was dead, but his son Archelaus now ruled the territory and had already shown himself capable of continuing his father's brutal policies. Joseph preferred to take their chances with Herod Antipas in Galilee rather than with Archelaus in Judea.

Beyond these concerns, Joseph was outspoken in his preference for Galilee as simply a better place to rear and educate a child. It required three weeks to overcome Mary's objections, but by the first of October Joseph had convinced her and all their friends that it was best for the family to return to Nazareth.

Accordingly, early in October of 4 B.C., they departed from Bethlehem, traveling by way of Lydda and Scythopolis. They set out early one Sunday morning, Mary and the child riding on their newly acquired beast of burden while Joseph and five accompanying kinsmen proceeded on foot. Joseph's relatives had refused to permit them to make the trip alone, fearing the dangers of the road for two travelers with a young child. They avoided the route through Jerusalem and the Jordan valley, taking instead the western roads that were considered somewhat safer, though still not without risk.

On the fourth day, the party reached Nazareth safely. They arrived unannounced at the family home, which had been occupied for more than three years by one of Joseph's married brothers. The brother was surprised to see them, for the family had conducted their affairs so quietly that neither Joseph's relatives nor Mary's people even knew they had left Alexandria. The next day, Joseph's brother moved his family out, and Mary, for the first time since Jesus's birth, was able to settle down with her little family to enjoy life in their own home.

Jesus was approximately three years and two months old at the time of their return to Nazareth. He had weathered all these travels remarkably well and was in excellent health, full of childish excitement at having a home of his own to explore. But he greatly missed the companionship of his Alexandrian playmates, and it would take time for him to form new friendships in Galilee.

On the journey to Nazareth, Joseph had persuaded Mary that it would be unwise to spread word among their Galilean friends and relatives that Jesus was a child of promise. They agreed to refrain from mentioning these matters to anyone. Both parents kept this promise faithfully throughout the years that followed, allowing their son to grow up without the burden of expectations that public knowledge of his special status would have created.

The family's fourth year in Nazareth was a period of normal physical development and unusual mental activity for Jesus. During this time he formed a close attachment to a neighbor boy about his own age named Jacob. The two were always happy in their play, and they grew up to be great friends and loyal companions. This friendship was Jesus's first significant relationship outside his immediate family, and it marked an important step in his social development.

In the early morning hours of April 2, 3 B.C., the second child of Joseph and Mary was born—a boy they named James. Jesus was thrilled at the thought of having a baby brother, and he would stand by the hour watching the infant's early activities. The arrival of James began the expansion of what would eventually become a large family, and it gave Jesus his first experiences with the dynamics of sibling relationships.

That same summer, Joseph built a small workshop close to the village spring and near the caravan stopping place. This location was strategic—the spring drew travelers and townspeople alike, and the caravan traffic brought potential customers from throughout the region. After establishing this shop, Joseph did little carpentry work for daily wages. Instead, he had two of his brothers and several other mechanics working for him while he remained at the shop making yokes and plows and doing other woodwork. He also worked with leather, rope, and canvas, gradually building a modest but stable business.

As Jesus grew, he divided his time about equally between helping his mother with home duties and watching his father work at the shop. The workshop became a place of education for the young boy, not merely in the carpenter's trade but in the wider ways of the world. He listened to the conversations of caravan conductors and travelers who stopped at the nearby spring, absorbing information about distant lands and diverse peoples from the four corners of the earth.

In July of this year, one month before Jesus turned four, an outbreak of malignant intestinal illness spread through Nazareth from contact with caravan travelers. Mary became so alarmed by the danger to Jesus that she bundled up both her children and fled to the country home of her brother, several miles south of Nazareth on the Megiddo road near the village of Sarid. They did not return to Nazareth for more than two months. Jesus greatly enjoyed this experience—his first extended stay on a farm—and it awakened in him an appreciation for rural life that would remain throughout his years.

In August of that year, Jesus turned five. Shortly before his birthday, he was made very happy by the arrival of his sister Miriam, born on the night of July 11. The evening following her birth, Joseph sat down with his son and had a long talk about the manner in which various groups of living things are born into the world as separate individuals. This conversation marked the beginning of what would become one of the most valuable aspects of Jesus's early education—the habit of learning through thoughtful questioning and patient parental explanation.

From the time Jesus was five years old until he was ten, he was one continuous question mark. Joseph and Mary could not always answer his questions, but they never failed to discuss his inquiries fully and to assist him in every possible way to reach satisfactory solutions to the problems his alert mind suggested.

The Jewish homes of Galilee in those days provided a structured program for child-rearing that few gentile households could match in intellectual, moral, and religious training. Children's lives were divided into clearly defined stages: the newborn child of the first eight days, the suckling child, the weaned child, the period of dependence on the mother lasting through the fifth year, and then the beginning of the child's independence, with the father assuming responsibility for a son's education.

According to this custom, on August 21, 2 B.C.—his fifth birthday—Mary formally turned Jesus over to Joseph for further instruction. Though Joseph now assumed direct responsibility for Jesus's intellectual and religious education, Mary continued to involve herself in his home training. She taught him to know and care for the vines and flowers growing about the garden walls that surrounded their home. She also provided shallow boxes of sand on the roof of the house—the family's summer bedroom—in which Jesus worked out maps and practiced his early writing in Aramaic, Greek, and eventually Hebrew. In time he learned to read, write, and speak all three languages fluently, an accomplishment that would later prove invaluable in his teaching ministry.

By every physical measure, Jesus appeared to be a nearly perfect child, continuing to make normal progress mentally and emotionally. He experienced a mild digestive upset toward the end of this fifth year—his first minor illness—but otherwise his health remained excellent. Though Joseph and Mary often talked privately about the future of their eldest child, an observer would have seen only a normal, healthy, carefree, but exceedingly inquisitive child of that time and place.

Jesus's sixth year brought several significant developments. With his mother's help, he had already mastered the Galilean dialect of Aramaic, and now his father began teaching him Greek. Joseph was a fluent speaker of both languages, while Mary spoke little Greek. Their textbook was the precious copy of the Hebrew scriptures in Greek—the Septuagint—that had been presented to them when they left Egypt. There were only two complete copies of the scriptures in Greek in all of Nazareth, and the possession of one by the carpenter's family made Joseph's home a much-sought place. As Jesus grew, he would meet an almost endless procession of earnest students and sincere truth seekers who came to consult this rare manuscript.

Before the year ended, Jesus had assumed custody of this priceless book, having been told on his sixth birthday that it had been presented to him by the Alexandrian friends and relatives. Within a short time, he could read it readily.

The first great shock of Jesus's young life occurred when he was not quite six years old. It had seemed to the boy that his father—or at least his father and mother together—knew everything. When a mild earthquake shook Nazareth one day, Jesus asked his father what had caused it. Joseph's honest answer transformed something fundamental in the child's understanding: "My son, I really do not know." Thus began a long and disconcerting process of discovery through which Jesus gradually learned that his earthly parents were not all-wise and all-knowing.

Joseph's first impulse had been to tell Jesus that God had caused the earthquake, but a moment's reflection warned him that such an answer would immediately provoke further and more difficult questions. Even at this early age, it was very hard to answer Jesus's questions by attributing things to God or the devil. In keeping with common Jewish belief, Jesus was long willing to accept the doctrine of good and evil spirits as explanations for mental and spiritual phenomena, but he very early became doubtful that such unseen influences were responsible for the physical events of the natural world.

Before Jesus was six years old, in the early summer of 1 B.C., Zacharias and Elizabeth and their son John came to visit the Nazareth family. Jesus and John had a happy time during this, their first visit within their memories. Though the visitors could remain only a few days, the parents talked over many things, including their plans for their sons' futures. While they were thus engaged, the boys played with blocks in the sand on the rooftop and enjoyed themselves in many other ways.

Having met John, who came from near Jerusalem, Jesus began to show unusual interest in the history of Israel and to inquire in detail about the meaning of Sabbath rites, synagogue sermons, and the recurring feasts of commemoration. Joseph explained the meaning of all these observances—the midwinter festival of lights commemorating the dedication of the temple after the restoration of the Mosaic services, the early springtime celebration of Purim honoring Esther and Israel's deliverance through her, the solemn Passover, the feast of first-fruits, and the most solemn of all, the feast of the new year and the day of atonement. While some of these celebrations were difficult for his young mind to fully understand, Jesus pondered them seriously and entered joyfully into the feast of tabernacles, the annual vacation season when Jewish families camped in leafy booths and devoted themselves to celebration.

During this year, Joseph and Mary had repeated difficulty with Jesus about his prayers. He insisted on talking to his heavenly Father much as he would talk to Joseph, his earthly father. This departure from the solemn and reverent ways of addressing God troubled his traditional parents, especially his mother. But there was no persuading the child to change. He would say his prayers just as he had been taught, after which he insisted on having "just a little talk with my Father in heaven." This early tendency to distinguish between formal religious observance and personal spiritual communion foreshadowed a theme that would characterize his entire life and teaching.

In June of this year, Joseph turned the Nazareth shop over to his brothers and formally entered upon his work as a building contractor. Before the year was over, the family income had more than tripled. Never again, until after Joseph's death, would the Nazareth family experience real poverty. The family continued to grow, and they spent considerable money on extra education and travel, but Joseph's increasing income always kept pace with their expanding needs.

The next few years saw Joseph doing considerable construction work at Cana, Bethlehem of Galilee, Magdala, Nain, Sepphoris, Capernaum, and Endor, as well as much building in and near Nazareth. As James grew old enough to help his mother with housework and care of the younger children, Jesus began making frequent trips with his father to these surrounding towns and villages. He was a keen observer, and he gained much practical knowledge from these journeys. He was diligently gathering information about how people lived and worked in the various regions of his homeland.

This year also saw Jesus make great progress in adjusting his strong feelings and vigorous impulses to the demands of family cooperation and home discipline. Mary was a loving mother but a fairly strict disciplinarian. In many ways, however, Joseph exerted the greater influence over Jesus, for it was his practice to sit down with the boy and fully explain the real and underlying reasons for disciplinary restrictions. Once a situation had been explained to him, Jesus was always intelligently and willingly cooperative with parental wishes and family rules. He was beginning to develop that remarkable capacity for understanding human motivations that would later characterize his dealings with all people.

Much of his spare time—when his mother did not require his help about the house—Jesus spent studying flowers and plants by day and the stars by night. He developed a habit that would sometimes concern his parents: lying on his back and gazing up into the starry heavens long after his usual bedtime, contemplating the vastness of creation with a wondering mind.

By the time Jesus was ready to begin his formal education at age seven, he had already acquired an impressive foundation. He was fluent in two languages and progressing in a third. He had traveled more widely than most Galilean children of his age. He had experienced life in a sophisticated metropolis, on a working farm, and in a small village. He had been exposed to people of diverse backgrounds through the caravan traffic near his father's shop. He possessed a complete copy of the scriptures and had already begun to read them. Most importantly, he had developed the habit of thoughtful inquiry and the expectation that questions deserved genuine answers rather than appeals to authority or tradition.

In August of this seventh year—the age when Jewish children were expected to begin their formal studies—Jesus entered the synagogue school at Nazareth. He was already a fluent reader, writer, and speaker of Aramaic and Greek. Now he was to learn Hebrew and to acquaint himself with the deeper study of the sacred law. He approached this new phase of his education with genuine eagerness, unaware that his penetrating questions would soon create considerable difficulty for his teachers, his parents, and ultimately himself.

The early years were complete. The helpless infant born in a stable beneath a Bethlehem inn, who had survived Herod's massacre and lived as an exile in Egypt, who had made the long journey back to Galilee and grown through the stages of early childhood—this child was about to enter a new phase of development. The years of formal education lay ahead, years that would further shape the mind that would one day articulate the most influential teachings in human history.

But for now, he was simply a bright, inquisitive, remarkably well-adjusted seven-year-old boy, the eldest son of a carpenter and his wife, beginning school in an obscure Galilean village. Nothing about him suggested anything extraordinary to casual observers. The other children in Nazareth saw only a playmate. The teachers at the synagogue school would see an unusually capable but sometimes troublesome student. His parents knew more, but even they could not fully comprehend what was unfolding within their firstborn child.

The true nature of Jesus of Nazareth remained hidden, as it would remain for many years to come. The world was not yet ready to recognize who walked among them, learning the carpenter's trade, studying the scriptures, asking endless questions, and gazing at the stars—wondering, perhaps, about the universe of which this small planet was such a tiny part.[1]

4

THE SCHOOL YEARS

The synagogue school at Nazareth followed a curriculum common throughout Jewish Palestine, yet the education Jesus received there was shaped by circumstances that made it distinctly valuable. Had he remained in Alexandria, his instruction would have been directed entirely by Jews along exclusively Jewish lines. In Nazareth, the diversity of the caravan trade and the influence of nearby Greek cities gave him exposure to gentile thought that would have been impossible in a more insular environment. The liberal character of the Nazareth synagogue, under the influence of the renowned teacher Jose, allowed for a breadth of inquiry that more conservative schools would never have tolerated.

Jesus had entered elementary school at age seven, already fluent in Aramaic and Greek and possessing his own copy of the scriptures. The curriculum centered on the Hebrew language and the sacred texts, with students progressing through increasingly complex material over six years—three years of elementary instruction followed by three years of advanced study. From the beginning, Jesus distinguished himself as an unusually capable student, though his penetrating questions sometimes created difficulties for his teachers.

His ninth year brought the first serious trouble at school. Jesus had always delighted in drawing landscapes and modeling objects in potter's clay—activities strictly forbidden by Jewish interpretation of the second commandment's prohibition against graven images. His parents had gradually permitted these pursuits at home, but the situation came to a crisis when a slower student discovered Jesus drawing a charcoal portrait of the teacher on the schoolroom floor.

The elders assembled to confront Joseph about his son's lawlessness. This was not the first complaint they had brought, but it was the most serious accusation yet lodged against the boy. Jesus listened to the indictment for some time, seated on a large stone outside the back door of his home. When they began blaming his father for these alleged misdeeds, he could bear it no longer. He marched inside and fearlessly confronted his accusers.

The elders were thrown into confusion. Some found the episode almost humorous, while others considered the boy sacrilegious if not blasphemous. Joseph stood speechless while Mary grew indignant. But Jesus insisted on being heard. He defended his viewpoint with remarkable self-possession for a child his age, and concluded by announcing that he would abide by whatever decision his father made. The committee departed in silence.

Mary tried to arrange a compromise—Jesus could continue his modeling at home if he promised to refrain from such activities at school. But Joseph felt compelled to uphold the rabbinical interpretation. From that day forward, as long as he lived in his father's house, Jesus never again drew or modeled the likeness of anything. He remained unconvinced that what he had done was wrong, and surrendering this favorite pastime constituted one of the great trials of his young life. But he submitted to his father's ruling without further protest.

In late June of that year, Jesus climbed Mount Tabor for the first time, accompanying his father to the summit on a clear day. The view was extraordinary—the boy felt he could see the entire world spread before him, or at least all the world he knew. The Sea of Galilee glittered to the east, the Mediterranean shimmered in the distant west, and the great plain of Esdraelon stretched below like a vast green carpet. It was a moment of expansion, a glimpse of horizons far beyond Nazareth.

That September, his second sister Martha was born. Three weeks later, Joseph began an addition to their house—a combined workshop and bedroom that would prove enormously significant for Jesus's development. A small workbench was built specifically for the boy, and for the first time he possessed tools of his own. Over the following years, he worked at this bench whenever time permitted and became highly skilled in making yokes—a craft that would later provide powerful imagery for his teaching.

The winter that followed was one of the coldest in Nazareth's memory. Jesus had seen snow on the distant mountains before, and occasionally a dusting had fallen on Nazareth itself, but this winter brought ice—something he had never experienced. The fact that water could exist as solid, liquid, and vapor fascinated him. He had long pondered the steam rising from boiling pots, and now he thought deeply about the physical constitution of the natural world.

In May he helped with the grain harvest on his uncle's farm for the first time. This began a pattern of practical education that would continue throughout his youth. Before reaching thirteen, Jesus had learned something about virtually every occupation practiced around Nazareth—farming, fishing, shepherding, and various crafts. The only trade he did not explore during these years was metalworking, though he would spend several months in a smith's shop after his father's death.

When work was slow, Joseph took his son on trips to nearby towns—Cana, Endor, Nain, and especially Sepphoris, the capital of Galilee, located only three miles northwest of Nazareth. These journeys gave Jesus invaluable exposure to the wider world. He visited his uncle's farm regularly and occasionally traveled to Magdala for fishing excursions. Each trip broadened his understanding and gave him perspective on his own family.

By his tenth year, Jesus had become the acknowledged leader of a group of seven Nazareth boys who banded together to promote achievements in physical, intellectual, and religious development. He introduced new games and improved methods of physical recreation, channeling his companions' energies toward more purposeful activities. He was a natural teacher who instinctively guided others, even when supposedly engaged in play.

On a July Sabbath early in his tenth year, while walking through the countryside with his father, Jesus first gave expression to feelings and ideas indicating an emerging awareness of the unusual nature of his life mission. Joseph listened attentively but offered little comment. The next day, Jesus had a similar but longer conversation with his mother. Mary likewise listened but volunteered no information. Nearly two years would pass before Jesus spoke again to his parents about this growing inner revelation concerning his identity and purpose.

That August he entered the advanced division of the synagogue school. His questions now created constant turbulence—he kept all Nazareth in a state of mild uproar with his persistent inquiries. His parents were reluctant to forbid the questions, and his chief teacher found himself intrigued rather than offended by the boy's curiosity, insight, and hunger for knowledge.

His playmates noticed nothing supernatural about him. In most respects he was like themselves, though his interest in study exceeded the average. His most unusual trait was his unwillingness to fight for his rights. Despite being well-developed physically for his age, he showed no inclination to defend himself even when treated unjustly or subjected to personal abuse. This might have caused him considerable suffering except for his friendship with Jacob, the stone mason's son who lived nearby.

Jacob, a year older than Jesus, appointed himself his friend's protector. Several times, older and rougher youths attacked Jesus, expecting easy victory over someone known for refusing to fight. They invariably met swift retribution from Jacob, who made it his business to ensure no one imposed on Jesus because of his peaceful nature. The friendship between the two boys deepened into one of the most important relationships of Jesus's youth.

This year Jesus began showing marked preference for the company of older persons. He delighted in discussing cultural, educational, social, economic, political, and religious matters with adult minds, and his depth of reasoning so impressed his elders that they were always willing to engage with him. His parents constantly tried to steer him toward companions closer to his own age, but Jesus gravitated persistently toward those who could teach him more.

Late in his tenth year, Jesus spent two months fishing with his uncle on the Sea of Galilee. He proved remarkably successful and became an expert fisherman well before reaching manhood. This experience, combined with his growing skill at carpentry, began shaping his thoughts about his future livelihood. After his first extended fishing trip, he had nearly decided to become a fisherman. But close association with his father's work gradually drew him toward carpentry, and eventually a combination of influences would lead him to become a religious teacher unlike any before him.

Joseph used these years to instruct his son in the diverse means of earning a living, explaining the relative advantages of agriculture, industry, and trade. Galilee was a more beautiful and prosperous region than Judea, with living costs roughly one-fourth those of Jerusalem. The province contained more than two hundred towns exceeding five thousand inhabitants and thirty with populations above fifteen thousand. It was a land of agricultural villages and thriving industrial cities, and Jesus absorbed everything he could learn about how its people lived and worked.

The eleventh year brought significant changes. Jesus continued his trips with Joseph and his visits to his uncle's farm, but he also spent considerable time at the caravan supply shop near the village spring. There, conversing with travelers from all parts of the known world, he acquired an astonishing store of information about international affairs. This was the last year in which he enjoyed much free play and youthful joy. From this time forward, difficulties and responsibilities multiplied rapidly.

In late June, his brother Jude was born under circumstances that proved nearly catastrophic. Complications attended the birth, and Mary became so seriously ill that she remained bedridden for several weeks. Joseph stayed home from work to help, and Jesus found himself occupied with endless errands and household duties. From the time of his mother's illness—just before he turned eleven—he was compelled to assume responsibilities that should not normally have fallen on him for another year or two. The carefree days of childhood were ending.

The chazan of the synagogue, recognizing Jesus's exceptional promise, began spending one evening each week helping him master the Hebrew scriptures. This teacher was greatly interested in his pupil's progress and assisted him in many ways. Yet he could never understand why Jesus showed no interest in pursuing advanced studies in Jerusalem under the learned rabbis. The boy listened politely to such suggestions but never seriously considered them.

About the middle of May, Joseph took Jesus on a business trip to Scythopolis, the chief Greek city of the Decapolis. This was the ancient Hebrew city of Beth-shean, now thoroughly Hellenized. On the journey, Joseph recounted the history associated with this region —the tragic story of King Saul, the wars with the Philistines, and the turbulent events of Israel's past. Jesus had often gazed at Scythopolis from the hills above Nazareth, curious about its extensive public works and ornate buildings, but his father had always avoided discussing the place.

Now they walked its streets together, and Jesus was deeply impressed. The clean appearance and orderly arrangement of this supposedly pagan city amazed him. He marveled at the open-air amphitheater and admired the beautiful marble temple dedicated to pagan gods. Joseph grew increasingly uncomfortable with his son's enthusiasm and tried to redirect his attention to the superior beauty and grandeur of the Jewish temple in Jerusalem.

As it happened, the annual competitive games between the Greek cities of the Decapolis were being held during their visit. Jesus begged his father to take him to see the athletic contests, pleading so insistently that Joseph reluctantly agreed. The boy was thrilled by what he witnessed—the demonstrations of physical development and athletic skill captivated him completely. Joseph watched in dismay as his son entered wholeheartedly into the spirit of these exhibitions of what he considered pagan vanity.

After the games concluded, Jesus expressed approval of what he had seen and suggested that young men in Nazareth would benefit from similar wholesome outdoor activities. Joseph launched into a lengthy explanation of why such practices were evil and contrary to Jewish values, but he could see that his son remained unconvinced.

That night, in their room at the inn, came the only time Jesus ever saw his father truly angry with him. In the course of their continued discussion, the boy forgot himself so completely that he suggested they return home and work to build an amphitheater in Nazareth. Joseph forgot his usual calm demeanor. Seizing Jesus by the shoulder, he exclaimed with barely contained fury that he must never again give utterance to such an evil thought.

Jesus was stunned. He had never before experienced the sting of his father's anger and was shocked beyond words. He replied simply, "Very well, my father, it shall be so." And never again, as long as Joseph lived, did Jesus allude even slightly to Greek athletics or the games he had witnessed. He learned something important that night about the boundaries of his father's tolerance, and though he remained inwardly unconvinced, he kept his convictions to himself.

Years later, Jesus would see the Greek amphitheater in Jerusalem and come to understand more fully how hateful such things were from the traditional Jewish perspective. Nevertheless, throughout his life he endeavored to incorporate wholesome recreation into his activities, and eventually into the program he established for his closest followers, as far as Jewish practice would permit.

At the end of this eleventh year, Jesus was vigorous, well-developed, moderately humorous, and fairly lighthearted. But increasingly he was given to periods of profound meditation and serious contemplation. He thought often about how to fulfill his obligations to his family while also answering what he sensed was a call to a larger mission. Already he had begun to conceive that his work would not be limited to the Jewish people alone.

His twelfth year proved eventful in many ways. He continued excelling at school and pursuing his study of nature, while also investigating with growing interest the various methods by which people earned their living. He began doing regular work in the home carpenter shop and was given an unusual privilege for a Jewish family —permission to manage his own earnings. This year he also learned the wisdom of keeping certain matters private. Having caused so much trouble in the village with his questions and unconventional views, he became increasingly discreet in concealing anything that might mark him as different from his peers.

Throughout this year he experienced many seasons of uncertainty, even doubt, about the nature of his mission. His naturally developing human mind did not yet fully grasp his dual nature. The fact that he possessed a single personality made it difficult to recognize the double origin of the factors composing that personality. He was working out profound questions that most humans never face, and he had no one with whom he could discuss them.

His relationships with his siblings improved notably during this period. He grew increasingly tactful, always compassionate and considerate of their welfare. He got along excellently with James, Miriam, and the younger children still to come. His relationship with Martha was generally good. Most of his domestic friction arose with Joseph and Jude, particularly the latter—personality conflicts that would persist for years.

This year Jesus paid more attention than ever to music and continued teaching the home school for his younger siblings. He became keenly conscious of the difference between his parents' viewpoints regarding his future. He often lay awake listening to their discussions when they thought him asleep. More and more he inclined toward his father's view that his mission would be spiritual rather than political, and Mary was increasingly hurt by the realization that her son was rejecting her guidance in matters concerning his life's direction. This breach of understanding would only widen as the years passed.

During his final year at the synagogue school, Jesus raised an issue that illustrated both his developing theological insight and his characteristic courage. He questioned his father about the Jewish custom of touching the mezuzah—the small parchment scroll affixed to the doorpost—each time one entered or left the house, then kissing the finger that had touched it while reciting a blessing. His parents had repeatedly explained why images and drawings were forbidden, warning that such things could be used for idolatrous purposes. Jesus, possessing a keen sense of consistency, pointed out that this habitual reverence toward a doorpost parchment seemed essentially idolatrous by the same reasoning. Joseph, recognizing the validity of the argument, removed the parchment from their doorpost.

This was one small example of a larger pattern. As time passed, Jesus modified many of his family's religious practices, including the traditional prayers and various customs. Such changes were possible in Nazareth because its synagogue operated under the influence of a liberal school of rabbis. But the process caused Jesus considerable inner distress. Throughout this year and the two that followed, he struggled constantly to adjust his personal convictions to the established beliefs of his parents.

Two great commands warred within him. One said: Be loyal to the highest convictions of truth and righteousness. The other said: Honor your father and mother, who have given you life and nurtured you. He never shirked the responsibility of making daily adjustments between these competing loyalties, and gradually he achieved a harmonious balance—a concept of group solidarity based on loyalty, fairness, tolerance, and love that allowed him to remain true to his deepest convictions while fulfilling his obligations to his family.

As the year progressed, Jesus's graduation from the synagogue school approached. On the first day of the week, March 20, A.D. 7, he completed the prescribed course of training and was pronounced a "son of the commandment"—a full member of the religious community with all the rights and responsibilities that status entailed. His teacher expressed confidence that this bright and dedicated student was destined for some outstanding career. Even the elders, despite all their difficulties with his nonconformist tendencies, were proud of the boy and had begun discussing plans to send him to Jerusalem for advanced study at the renowned Hebrew academies.

Jesus listened to these plans but grew increasingly certain he would never study with the rabbis in Jerusalem. He sensed that his path lay in a different direction, though he could not yet clearly see where it would lead. What he did not know was that circumstances would soon make such plans impossible regardless of anyone's wishes. Tragedy was approaching that would transform him from a student into the head of a household, forcing him to assume responsibilities for which no education could have fully prepared him.

Joseph had come from Sepphoris, where he was supervising construction of a new public building, to be present for his son's graduation. It was a day of celebration and hope. The family could not have imagined that within a year, Joseph would be dead and everything would change. For now, they rejoiced in this milestone, proud of their eldest son's accomplishments and dreaming of the bright future that surely awaited him.

The boy who had survived Herod's massacre and grown up in the obscurity of Nazareth had completed his formal education. He could read and write three languages fluently. He had mastered the Hebrew scriptures and absorbed the teachings of the rabbis. He had learned carpentry from his father, fishing from his uncle, and farming from his relatives. He had traveled more widely than most Galilean youths and conversed with people from distant lands. He had formed his own views on matters religious, social, and political—views he had learned to keep largely to himself.

At twelve years old, standing on the threshold of Jewish manhood, Jesus of Nazareth was as prepared as any human being could be for what lay ahead. Yet even he could not have anticipated how drastically his life was about to change, or how quickly the dreams of further education and gradual preparation would give way to the harsh demands of premature responsibility.[1]

5

THE FIRST PASSOVER

WOMEN WERE NOT REQUIRED TO ATTEND THE PASSOVER FEAST IN Jerusalem, and most families left their wives and daughters behind when they made the pilgrimage. But Jesus virtually refused to go unless his mother accompanied them. When Mary decided to make the journey, her example inspired many other Nazareth women to join the caravan, so that the company departing that year contained the largest proportion of women ever to travel from Nazareth to the Passover.

The Passover of A.D. 7 fell on Saturday, April 9. A company of one hundred and three pilgrims assembled in Nazareth early Monday morning, April 4, to begin the journey. They had little to fear in taking Jesus to Jerusalem. The dreaded Archelaus had been deposed, and twelve years had passed since the first Herod sought to destroy the infant of Bethlehem. No one would think to connect that ancient affair with this obscure boy from Nazareth.

The Nazareth party followed the eastern route through the Jordan valley—the same path Joseph and Mary had traveled years before. But everything felt different now. Jesus walked among a company of over a hundred pilgrims, their voices rising in the traditional psalms of ascent as they made their way south. He listened as his parents pointed out landmarks along the way, though he said little, absorbing the experience of his first journey to the holy city.

The four-day journey passed quickly. On the evening before the final day of travel, the caravan stopped at Jericho, where Jesus walked with his parents to the site of ancient Jericho—where Joshua, for whom he was named, had performed his renowned exploits according to Jewish tradition.

On the eastern slopes of Olivet, they paused at the village of Bethany, where they were welcomed by a man named Simon whose three children—Mary, Martha, and Lazarus—were close to Jesus's age. A friendship formed that day between the two households, one that would prove significant in the years ahead.

From the crest of Olivet, Jesus saw Jerusalem for the first time—at least the first time he could remember—the holy city spread before him, the imposing palaces gleaming in the afternoon sun, and the inspiring temple of his Father rising above them all. At no time in his entire life did Jesus experience such a purely human thrill as that which completely enthralled him as he stood there on this April afternoon. Years later, on this same spot, he would stand and weep over the city that was about to reject another prophet—the last and greatest of her heavenly teachers.

They hurried on into Jerusalem. It was Thursday afternoon, and never had Jesus beheld such throngs of human beings. He meditated deeply on how Jews had assembled here from the farthest corners of the known world. They made their way to a large home belonging to a well-to-do relative of Mary who knew something of the early history of both John and Jesus through Zacharias. There the family would stay during Passover week.

The following day, the day of preparation, they made ready for the Passover Sabbath. Joseph found time to take his son to visit the academy where arrangements had been made for Jesus to resume his education at age fifteen. Joseph was puzzled when the boy showed little interest in these carefully laid plans. Jesus was too absorbed in his own thoughts to ask many questions—a striking departure from his usual behavior.

His first visit to the temple profoundly impressed him, but not in the way his parents had anticipated. From the Mount of Olives and from outside its walls, the temple had been everything Jesus expected and more. But when he entered its sacred precincts, disillusionment began.

In company with his parents, Jesus passed through the temple courts on his way to join the group of new sons of the law who were to be consecrated as full citizens of Israel. He was somewhat disappointed by the general demeanor of the temple crowds, but the first great shock came when his mother left them to take her place in the women's gallery. It had never occurred to Jesus that his mother would be excluded from the consecration ceremonies. He was thoroughly indignant that she was made to suffer such unjust discrimination. Though he made a few remarks of protest to his father, he said nothing more at the time. But he thought deeply, as his questions to the scribes and teachers a week later would reveal.

The consecration rituals themselves disappointed him. They seemed perfunctory and routine, lacking the personal warmth that character-ized the ceremonies at the Nazareth synagogue. Afterward, he returned to greet his mother and then accompanied his father on a tour of the temple's courts, galleries, and corridors. The precincts could accommodate more than two hundred thousand worshipers at once, and while the vastness of these buildings—far greater than anything he had ever seen—impressed his mind, he was more intrigued by contemplating the spiritual significance of the cere-monies and their associated worship.

Many of the temple rituals touched his sense of the beautiful and the symbolic, but he was consistently disappointed by the explanations his parents offered when he asked about their deeper meanings. Jesus simply could not accept interpretations of worship that involved belief in the wrath of God or the anger of the Almighty. Later, when his father became mildly insistent that he acknowledge the orthodox Jewish beliefs about divine judgment, Jesus turned suddenly to his parents. Looking appealingly into his father's eyes, he said: "My father, it cannot be true—the Father in heaven cannot regard his erring children on earth in such a way. The heavenly Father cannot love his children less than you love me. And I know well that no matter what unwise thing I might do, you would never pour out wrath upon me or vent anger against me. If you, my earthly father, possess such human reflections of the Divine, how much more must the heavenly Father be filled with goodness and overflowing with mercy. I refuse to believe that my Father in heaven loves me less than my father on earth."

Joseph and Mary heard these words from their firstborn son and held their peace. Never again did they attempt to change his mind about the love of God and the mercifulness of the Father in heaven.

Everywhere Jesus went throughout the temple courts, he was disturbed by the spirit of irreverence he observed. The conduct of the crowds seemed inconsistent with their presence in what he thought of as his Father's house. But the greatest shock came when Joseph escorted him into the court of the gentiles. There he encountered a scene of chaos—loud talking and cursing, the bleating of sheep, the babble of the money-changers and vendors of sacrificial animals, and the commerce in various other commodities. His sense of propriety was most outraged by the sight of frivolous women parading through the temple precinct—painted courtesans of the type he had seen in Sepphoris. This profanation aroused all his youthful indignation, and he did not hesitate to express himself freely to Joseph.

They descended to the priests' court beneath the rock ledge where the altar stood, to observe the killing of the sacrificial animals and the washing of blood from the hands of the officiating priests at the bronze fountain. The bloodstained pavement, the gory hands of the priests, and the sounds of dying animals proved more than this nature-loving boy could endure. The terrible sight sickened him. He clutched his father's arm and begged to be taken away. They walked back through the court of the gentiles, and even the coarse laughter and profane jesting he heard there came as relief from the horrors he had just witnessed.

Joseph saw how deeply the temple rites had affected his son and wisely led him around to view the Beautiful Gate, an artistic portal of Corinthian bronze. But Jesus had experienced enough for his first temple visit. They returned to the upper court for Mary and spent an hour walking in the open air, away from the crowds, viewing the Asmonean palace, the stately home of Herod, and the tower of the Roman guards. Joseph explained that only inhabitants of Jerusalem were permitted to witness the daily temple sacrifices; Galileans came only three times yearly—for Passover, Pentecost, and the feast of tabernacles.

Five Nazareth families joined Simon of Bethany's household for the Passover meal. It was the slaughter of the paschal lambs in such enormous numbers that had so affected Jesus during his temple visit. The original plan had been to celebrate with Mary's relatives in Jerusalem, but Jesus persuaded his parents to accept Simon's invitation to Bethany instead.

That evening they gathered for the ancient rites, eating roasted lamb with unleavened bread and bitter herbs. As a new son of the covenant, Jesus was asked to recount the origin of the Passover. He performed this duty well but somewhat disconcerted his parents by including remarks that reflected the impressions made on his thoughtful young mind by what he had recently witnessed. Even at this early date, Jesus had begun questioning whether the Father in heaven truly desired the slaughter of so many innocent animals. He felt assured in his own mind that such spectacles did not please God, and he became increasingly determined to someday establish a bloodless Passover celebration.

Jesus slept little that night. His rest was disturbed by revolting dreams of slaughter and suffering. His mind struggled with the inconsistencies and absurdities he perceived in the Jewish ceremonial system. His parents likewise slept poorly, deeply unsettled by the events of the day and their son's strange, determined attitude. Mary became nervously agitated, while Joseph, though equally puzzled, maintained his usual calm. Both feared to discuss these matters frankly with Jesus, though he would gladly have talked with them had they encouraged him.

The following day's services proved more acceptable, doing much to relieve the unpleasant memories. Young Lazarus then took Jesus in hand for a systematic exploration of Jerusalem and its environs. Jesus discovered the various places around the temple where teaching conferences were held, and aside from a few visits to gaze in wonder at the veil separating the holy of holies, he spent most of his time at these discussions.

Throughout Passover week, Jesus kept his place among the newly consecrated sons of the commandment, which meant sitting outside the rail that segregated those who were not full citizens of Israel. Conscious of his youth, he refrained from asking the many questions surging through his mind—at least until the Passover celebration ended and these restrictions were lifted.

On Wednesday of Passover week, Jesus spent the night at Simon's home in Bethany. That evening, Lazarus, Martha, and Mary listened as Jesus discussed matters temporal and eternal, human and divine. From that night forward, all three loved him as if he were their own brother.

Again and again during the week, his parents found Jesus sitting alone with his head in his hands, lost in profound thought. They had never seen him behave this way, and not understanding how confused and troubled he was by his experiences, they grew increasingly perplexed. They welcomed the passing of the Passover days and longed to have their strangely acting son safely home in Nazareth.

Day by day Jesus worked through his problems. By the week's end he had made many mental adjustments, but his mind still swarmed with perplexities and unanswered questions. Before leaving Jerusalem, Joseph and Mary, together with Jesus's Nazareth teacher, finalized arrangements for the boy to return at age fifteen for advanced studies at one of the most renowned rabbinical academies. Jesus accompanied his parents and teacher on their visits to the school, but they were all distressed by his apparent indifference to everything they said and did. Mary was deeply pained by his reactions to the Jerusalem visit, and Joseph was profoundly perplexed by his strange remarks and unusual conduct.

Yet the week had provided valuable experiences beyond the troubling ones. Jesus met scores of boys his own age, fellow candidates for consecration, and used these contacts to learn how people lived in Mesopotamia, Turkestan, Parthia, and the far western provinces of Rome. Thousands of young people had gathered in Jerusalem, and Jesus personally interviewed more than one hundred and fifty of them. He was particularly interested in those from distant eastern and western lands. These encounters planted in him a desire to someday travel the world and learn how different peoples earned their living.

The Nazareth party had arranged to gather near the temple at midmorning on the first day of the week after Passover ended. Jesus went into the temple to listen to the ongoing discussions while his parents awaited their fellow travelers. When the company assembled and prepared to depart, the men formed one group and the women another, as was customary for such journeys. Jesus had traveled to

Jerusalem with his mother among the women. Now, as a consecrated young man, he was expected to return with his father among the men.

But as the Nazareth party moved toward Bethany, Jesus remained completely absorbed in a temple discussion about angels, utterly unmindful that the time for departure had passed. He did not realize he had been left behind until the noon adjournment of the conference.

The travelers did not discover his absence until they reached Jericho and prepared to stop for the night. Mary had assumed he was journeying with the men; Joseph thought he was traveling with the women since he had come up to Jerusalem in their company. After inquiring among the last arrivals and learning that no one had seen their son, they spent a sleepless night wondering what had happened to him, recounting his unusual behavior during Passover week, and quietly reproaching each other for not ensuring he was present before they left Jerusalem.

Meanwhile, Jesus had remained in the temple throughout the afternoon, listening to the discussions. At their conclusion, he walked to Bethany, arriving as Simon's family sat down to their evening meal. The three young people were delighted to see him. He visited little that evening, spending most of his time alone in the garden, meditating.

Early the next morning, Jesus was up and on his way back to the temple. On the brow of Olivet he paused and wept—wept over the sight of a spiritually impoverished people, tradition-bound and living under Roman occupation. By early morning he had reached the temple with his mind made up to participate in the discussions.

Joseph and Mary had also risen at dawn, intending to retrace their steps to Jerusalem. They hurried first to the home where they had lodged during Passover week, but no one there had seen Jesus. After searching all day without finding any trace of him, they returned to spend another anxious night.

At the second day's conference, Jesus made bold to ask questions, participating in the temple discussions in an amazing manner yet always appropriate to his youth. His pointed questions sometimes embarrassed the learned teachers of Jewish law, but he displayed such candid fairness combined with evident hunger for knowledge that most of the teachers treated him with consideration.

When he presumed to question the justice of executing a drunken gentile who had accidentally wandered from the court of the gentiles into the forbidden inner precincts, one intolerant teacher lost patience. Glowering down at the boy, he demanded to know his age. Jesus replied that he was thirteen years old, lacking slightly more than four months. The teacher retorted that he had no business being there since he was not yet of legal age as a son of the law. When Jesus explained that he had received consecration during the Passover and was a finished student of the Nazareth schools, the teachers derisively replied that they might have known—he was from Nazareth. But the leader of the discussion ruled that Jesus was not to blame if the Nazareth synagogue had graduated him at twelve instead of thirteen. Despite several detractors walking out in protest, the boy was permitted to continue as a student in the discussions.

The third day drew many spectators who had heard about this youth from Galilee and came to see a boy confuse the wise men of the law. Simon came down from Bethany to watch. Throughout that day, Joseph and Mary continued their anxious search, even entering the temple several times but never thinking to examine the discussion groups—though once they passed almost within hearing distance of their son's voice.

Before the day ended, the entire attention of the chief discussion group had focused on Jesus's questions. Among them were these: What really exists in the holy of holies behind the veil? Why should mothers in Israel be segregated from male temple worshipers? If God is a father who loves his children, why all this slaughter of animals to gain divine favor—has the teaching of Moses been misunderstood? Since the temple is dedicated to worshiping the Father in heaven, is it consistent to permit those who engage in commerce and trade? Is the expected Messiah to become a temporal prince sitting on David's throne, or is he to function as the light of life in establishing a spiritual kingdom?

All day long, those who listened marveled at these questions. For more than four hours the Nazareth youth engaged the Jewish teachers with thought-provoking, heart-searching inquiries. He offered few comments on his elders' remarks, conveying his own teaching primarily through the questions he asked. By the deft and subtle phrasing of a question, he could simultaneously challenge their teaching and suggest his own views. His manner combined wisdom and humor in a way that endeared him even to those who resented his youth. He was always fair and considerate, exhibiting a reluctance to take unfair advantage that would characterize his entire later ministry. He seemed utterly free from any desire to win arguments merely for the satisfaction of logical triumph. He cared about only one thing: proclaiming everlasting truth and revealing more fully the character of the eternal God.

When the day ended, Simon and Jesus walked back to Bethany together, mostly in silence. Again Jesus paused on the brow of Olivet, but this time he did not weep. He only bowed his head in silent devotion. After the evening meal, he declined to join the family circle and went instead to the garden, where he lingered late into the night, struggling to formulate some definite plan for his lifework. How could he best reveal to his spiritually blinded countrymen a more beautiful concept of the heavenly Father? How could he set them free from their bondage to law, ritual, ceremony, and tradition? The clear light he sought did not come.

The next morning—the fourth day—Jesus seemed strangely unmindful of his earthly parents. When Lazarus's mother remarked at breakfast that his parents must be nearly home by now, Jesus appeared not to comprehend that they would be worried about his absence.

He journeyed again to the temple, this time without pausing to meditate on Olivet. The morning discussions focused on the law and the prophets, and the teachers were astonished by Jesus's familiarity with the scriptures in both Hebrew and Greek. They marveled not so much at his knowledge as at his youth.

At the afternoon conference, they had barely begun addressing his question about the purpose of prayer when the leader invited Jesus to come forward, sit beside him, and state his own views on prayer and worship.

That same evening, Joseph and Mary had heard about the strange youth who was so skillfully engaging the temple teachers, but it never occurred to them that this boy might be their son. They had nearly decided to journey to Zacharias's home, thinking Jesus might have gone there to visit Elizabeth and John. On the chance that Zacharias might be at the temple, they stopped there on their way. As they walked through the courts, imagine their astonishment when they recognized the voice of their missing son and saw him seated among the teachers.

Joseph stood speechless, but Mary released her long pent-up fear and anxiety. Rushing up to Jesus, who had risen to greet his startled parents, she exclaimed: "My child, why have you treated us like this? For more than three days your father and I have searched for you in sorrow. What possessed you to desert us?"

It was a tense moment. All eyes turned to hear what Jesus would say. His father looked at him reprovingly but remained silent.

Jesus was, by every measure, supposed to be a young man now. He had finished his schooling, been recognized as a son of the law, and received consecration as a citizen of Israel. Yet his mother had publicly upbraided him before the entire assembly, right in the midst of the most serious and sublime effort of his young life, bringing to an inglorious end one of the greatest opportunities he would ever be granted to function as a teacher of truth, a preacher of righteousness, a revealer of the loving character of his Father in heaven.

But the boy proved equal to the occasion. After a moment's thought, he answered his mother: "Why have you searched for me so long? Would you not expect to find me in my Father's house, since the time has come when I should be about my Father's business?"

Everyone was astonished at his manner of speaking. They silently withdrew, leaving him alone with his parents. The young man relieved the awkwardness by saying quietly: "Come, my parents. None has done anything but what seemed best to them. Our Father in heaven has ordained these things. Let us go home."

In silence they departed, arriving at Jericho for the night. Only once did they pause—on the brow of Olivet. There Jesus raised his staff aloft and, trembling from head to foot with intense emotion, declared: "O Jerusalem, Jerusalem, and the people thereof, what slaves you are— subservient to the Roman yoke and victims of your own traditions! But I will return to cleanse yonder temple and deliver my people from this bondage!"

During the three days' journey to Nazareth, Jesus said little, and his parents said little in his presence. They were at a loss to understand their firstborn son's conduct, but they treasured his words in their hearts, even when they could not fully comprehend their meaning.

Upon reaching home, Jesus made a brief statement to his parents, assuring them of his affection and implying that they need not fear he would again give them occasion for anxiety over his behavior. He concluded this momentous declaration by saying: "While I must do the will of my Father in heaven, I will also be obedient to my father on earth. I will await my hour."

Though Jesus would many times refuse inwardly to consent to his parents' well-intentioned but misguided efforts to dictate his thinking or establish plans for his work, he did most gracefully conform to his earthly father's wishes and to the usages of his family in every manner consistent with his dedication to doing his heavenly Father's will.

The boy who had questioned the teachers in the temple, who had wept over Jerusalem's spiritual blindness, who had declared his intention to return and cleanse the sacred precincts—this boy went home to Nazareth and resumed the quiet life of a carpenter's son. The great work would have to wait. His hour had not yet come.

But the seed had been planted. The questions he had asked would echo through the years. The vision he had glimpsed on the Mount of Olives—of a people freed from bondage to tradition and awakened to the true character of their heavenly Father—would never leave him. Everything that followed in his remarkable life flowed from what began during this single week in Jerusalem, when a boy of nearly thirteen first confronted the gap between what religion had become and what it was meant to be.[1]

6

THE DEATH OF JOSEPH

In the early autumn of A.D. 8, the future had never looked brighter for the family of Joseph and Mary. After years of careful management and steady work, their financial position had finally stabilized. The carpentry shop was thriving. The children were healthy. And Joseph had just made arrangements that filled him with quiet pride: he had set aside funds to eventually send Jesus to Jerusalem for formal education under the rabbis. The boy's brilliance was undeniable. His questions at the temple the previous spring had astonished even the learned teachers. Joseph intended to give his eldest son every opportunity to develop that remarkable mind.

Jesus had just celebrated his fourteenth birthday. He stood at the threshold of young manhood, still helping in the shop, still studying the scriptures, still wrestling privately with the growing awareness of his unusual nature. The household bustled with the energy of eight children. James was ten, Joseph eight, Simon seven, Martha nearly six, Jude four, Amos two, and Ruth was still in Mary's womb. It was a full house, a happy house, a house with plans.

Then came the runner from Sepphoris.

On the morning of September 25, Joseph had gone to work on the new residence being constructed for the Roman governor, just four miles from Nazareth. It was good work, well-paid, the kind of contract that would further secure his family's future. Shortly before noon, a derrick collapsed. Joseph was struck and critically injured.

A messenger was dispatched immediately to Nazareth. Jesus received the news first. He sent for his mother, and together they made the urgent journey to Sepphoris. Mary, five months pregnant, traveled as quickly as her condition would allow.

They arrived too late. Joseph had died from his injuries before Mary could reach his side.

There would be no final words between husband and wife. No farewell blessing. No last embrace. The man who had protected Mary through scandal and exile, who had raised Jesus as his own son while guarding the secret of his origin, who had built a life of dignity and devotion through the work of his hands—this man was gone. He was laid to rest with his fathers on September 26, A.D. 8.

Jesus stood at the graveside not as a grieving child but as the new head of his household.

The magnitude of what had befallen this family cannot be overstated. In a single day, a fourteen-year-old boy became the sole support of a pregnant widow and seven younger siblings. The education fund vanished into immediate necessities. The plans for Jerusalem evaporated. Every dream Joseph had carefully constructed was demolished by a falling beam in Sepphoris.

What followed would later be described as the most crucial period of Jesus's entire earthly existence—more testing than any temptation he would face in the wilderness, more demanding than any challenge of his public ministry. The real trial of the God-man was not forty days of fasting in the Judean desert. It was the years of grinding responsibility that began on this September day.

The family's circumstances deteriorated rapidly. Joseph had been owed money for recent work, but collecting debts proved difficult. The carpentry business required experienced hands to maintain its contracts, and while Jesus was skilled for his age, he was still a boy competing against established tradesmen. Savings were consumed. Luxuries disappeared. The comfortable home became merely adequate, then strained.

Through the autumn and winter, Jesus assumed his new role with remarkable composure. He managed the household accounts. He negotiated with creditors. He kept the shop operating as best he could while his mother recovered from the shock of her loss. He became father to his brothers and sisters in practice as well as responsibility.

On April 17 of the following year, A.D. 9, Mary gave birth to Ruth—the child Joseph would never see. Jesus delivered his baby sister himself, assisted by a neighboring woman. The family was now complete: a widow, a teenage provider, and eight children ranging from infant to eleven years old.

As Jesus approached his fifteenth year, he was called upon to deliver his first sermon at the Nazareth synagogue. This was customary for young men of his age, but Jesus's circumstances gave the occasion unusual weight. The community knew this family. They had watched Joseph's sudden death. They had seen the teenage boy holding everything together. Now they would hear him speak.

What Jesus delivered that Sabbath was not recorded in detail, but its effect was noted. He spoke with an authority that seemed beyond his years—not the borrowed authority of quoted rabbis, but something that appeared to arise from direct knowledge. The elders listened with growing attention. Here was Joseph's boy, barely fifteen, carrying burdens that would break many men, speaking of God as though he actually knew Him.

The sermon marked a subtle shift in how Nazareth regarded Jesus. He was no longer simply the promising son of a respected carpenter. He was becoming something harder to categorize—a young man of unusual depth, unusual composure, unusual presence.

The years between fourteen and sixteen tested Jesus more severely than any subsequent period of his life. Later tradition would focus on the wilderness temptation, with its dramatic confrontation between good and evil. But those forty days were a concentrated crisis. The real temptation was chronic, daily, relentless: the temptation to use powers he was beginning to recognize for purposes that would have eased his family's suffering but compromised his mission. The temptation to despair. The temptation to rage against the apparent cruelty of providence. The temptation to abandon the slow human path for shortcuts that his divine nature could easily provide.

He resisted all of them. Not in a single heroic moment, but through hundreds of ordinary days of choosing faithfulness over frustration, patience over power, trust over bitterness.

By his sixteenth birthday, Jesus had established himself as the head of the household. The family was not prosperous, but neither were they destitute. The younger children were fed, clothed, and taught. Mary had found her footing as a widow. The carpentry shop continued to operate.

Most remarkably, Jesus himself had not become hard or cynical. The grinding pressure had not crushed his spirit or corrupted his charac-ter. He emerged from these two crucial years with his humanity deep-ened rather than diminished, his compassion expanded by suffering, his understanding of human existence authenticated by experience.

When he would later speak to the poor, the grieving, the overburdened—he would speak as one who had lived among them. When he would teach about God's care for human needs, he would teach as one who had trusted that care through nights of genuine uncertainty. When he would offer comfort to those who had lost loved ones, he would offer it as one who had buried his own father and comforted his own mother.

The death of Joseph, terrible as it was, accomplished something in Jesus that no amount of study or privilege could have achieved. It grounded his divinity in genuine humanity. It gave God's Son the credentials of authentic human experience.

He was ready now for the next phase of his preparation—years that would bring new tests, new opportunities, and new revelations of who he was and why he had come.[1]

7

THE ZEALOT CRISIS

By his sixteenth year, Jesus had emerged from adolescence into young manhood. The transition was complete. He stood at his full physical stature now—a strong, vigorous young man with a presence that was somehow both commanding and gentle. His face was handsome, his movements assured, but there was nothing arrogant in his bearing. When he spoke, his voice carried a musical quality that held attention. When he listened, his eyes were kind but searching, as though he could see past words into intentions.

Those who met him invariably noticed something unusual. There seemed to be a duality in his nature—two dimensions occupying the same space. He was a sympathizing friend who could comfort a grieving neighbor, and simultaneously an authoritative teacher who spoke with inexplicable certainty about matters of the soul. Even in commonplace encounters—discussing the price of timber, negotiating a carpentry contract, settling a dispute between siblings—there was this peculiar quality of depth.

Jesus himself was becoming increasingly aware of the complexity of his situation. He carried within himself the consciousness of divinity—not fully articulated yet, not completely understood, but growing clearer with each passing month. He knew he was not destined to be what his mother hoped. He was not going to lead a nationalist rebellion or restore David's throne. He had something else to reveal, something more profound than political liberation, but he could not yet name it precisely even to himself.

The friction this created within his household was considerable. Mary had not abandoned her conviction that her eldest son would become the Messiah of Jewish expectation. She watched him work at the carpenter's bench day after day, saw his extraordinary abilities wasted on ordinary labor, and grieved. In her mind, he should have been in Jerusalem studying under the rabbis, preparing for his destined role. Instead, he was here in Nazareth, earning bread for his siblings.

Jesus rarely argued with her anymore. He had learned that no amount of explanation would shift her fundamental assumptions. His father Joseph had never been able to change her mind on these matters, and Jesus had inherited the same futility. So he simply let her believe what she would believe, and went about the quiet business of being a father to his brothers and sisters.

His performance was exemplary. The younger children adored him. He spent every free moment with them—teaching, playing, listening to their troubles, settling their disputes. He had transformed the household into something resembling a school, insisting that the girls receive the same education as the boys. This was unusual in Jewish families, but Jesus maintained it was right, and Mary agreed. So Miriam and Martha studied alongside their brothers, learning to read and reason and question.

Simon had started formal schooling this year, which meant selling another house to cover expenses. The family's finances remained precarious. Jesus worked constantly, producing carpentry of such superior quality that he was never idle, but there were many mouths to feed and bodies to clothe. James, now thirteen, had taken over teaching the younger children, freeing Jesus to spend more time at the workbench. The household functioned, but just barely.

Through it all, Jesus maintained an inner certainty about his future. He had decided that once his siblings were raised and married—once his responsibility to his father's household was fulfilled—he would enter upon his true work. He would be a teacher of living truth, a revealer of the heavenly Father. He did not know precisely what form this would take. He only knew it was coming.

But before that day arrived, his carefully maintained equilibrium would be severely tested.

The trouble began in his seventeenth year, arriving from Jerusalem with all the force of a political storm.

Throughout Judea and Galilee, nationalist sentiment was rising. The Jewish people had endured Roman occupation for decades, paying taxes to a foreign power, watching their religious sensibilities mocked by gentile overlords. Resentment had been building, and now it was finding organized expression. A movement was forming—soon to be called the Zealots—committed to armed rebellion. Unlike the Pharisees, who counseled patience and prayer for the Messiah's arrival, the Zealots intended to force the issue through military action.

Organizers from Jerusalem fanned out across the countryside, recruiting young men to the cause. When they reached Nazareth, they found fertile ground. The town was ready for revolution.

The organizers came to see Jesus. His reputation had preceded him. Here was the eldest son of Joseph, a young man of exceptional ability, respected throughout Nazareth, known for his wisdom and his way with words. If they could win Jesus to their cause, half the town's youth would follow.

They presented their case with passion: the oppression of Rome, the humiliation of God's chosen people, the necessity of action. They invoked scripture and prophecy. They appealed to his Jewish identity, his loyalty to his people, his duty to God.

Jesus listened carefully. He asked thoughtful questions. He gave them every courtesy.

Then he declined to join.

He offered no detailed explanation. He simply said no, politely but firmly, and the refusal confused everyone. Why would this promising young man reject such a righteous cause? The organizers left Nazareth puzzled and frustrated, and their confusion spread through the community.

Mary was horrified. Here was the opportunity she had been waiting for—her son stepping forward to lead his people, just as she had always believed he would. She pressed him hard, using every argument she could marshal. She even suggested that his refusal constituted disobedience to his parents, a violation of the promise he had made in Jerusalem to submit to their authority.

Jesus simply laid a gentle hand on her shoulder, looked into her face, and said quietly, 'My mother, how could you?'

Mary withdrew the accusation. But she did not understand.

The situation in Nazareth deteriorated rapidly. Jesus's refusal to join the Zealots created a schism among the town's young men. About half enlisted in the nationalist cause, following the lead of Simon—Mary's brother, Jesus's uncle—who had become an officer in the Galilean division. The other half formed an opposing group of more moderate patriots, and they wanted Jesus to lead them.

He refused that too.

This baffled everyone even more. If he wouldn't join the radicals, surely he would lead the moderates? It seemed the obvious compromise. But Jesus declined the honor, citing his family responsibilities. The moderates accepted this explanation reluctantly—everyone knew he was supporting a widowed mother and eight siblings—but they remained puzzled and disappointed.

Then Isaac stepped forward.

Isaac was a wealthy Jew who had made his fortune as a moneylender to gentiles—a profession that earned him both riches and social suspicion. He saw in Jesus the potential for something significant. Isaac made an extraordinary offer: he would support Jesus's entire family financially if Jesus would lay down his carpenter's tools and assume leadership of the Nazareth patriots.

Suddenly the family responsibility excuse evaporated. The moderates pressed their case with renewed intensity. Jesus's position became untenable.

He was barely seventeen years old, and he stood at the center of a political maelstrom. The entire town was divided. Mary, his uncle Simon, and even his younger brother James were all urging him to accept leadership. The better Jews of Nazareth had already enlisted in the nationalist cause. Those who had held back were waiting to see what Jesus would do. His decision would determine the town's political future.

And he could not tell them the truth.

He could not explain that he was more than a man. He could not disclose the mission that awaited him. He could not describe the revelation he was meant to bring—a revelation that had nothing to do with political liberation and everything to do with spiritual transformation. All of that was still forming, still clarifying, still years away from its proper time.

But he had to give them some answer.

Jesus had only one wise counselor in all this chaos: the chazan, his old teacher from the synagogue school. The chazan understood that Jesus carried something unusual within him, though he could not have named it. When the citizens' committee of Nazareth formally requested Jesus's response to their public appeal, the chazan advised him carefully.

This was the first time in Jesus's life that he had consciously resorted to what might be called public strategy. Until now, he had always relied on straightforward honesty. But straightforward honesty was impossible here. He could not reveal the full truth, yet he could not simply refuse without explanation. He had to find a way to satisfy legitimate concerns while protecting the mission he barely understood himself.

On the appointed day, Jesus stood before the assembled citizens and delivered his response.

He acknowledged the nationalist cause with respect. He praised the courage of those who had enlisted. He made it clear he was not criticizing their choice. But he restated, firmly and without apology, that his first duty was to his family. A widowed mother and eight brothers and sisters needed more than money could buy. They needed the care and guidance of a father, and a cruel accident had thrust that obligation upon him. He could not in clear conscience abandon them.

He paid tribute to his mother and eldest brother for their willingness to release him from this duty. But loyalty to his dead father, he said, forbade his leaving the family, regardless of how much financial support might be offered for their material needs.

Then he said something that would be remembered in Nazareth for years: 'Money cannot love.'

It was a simple statement, but it shifted the entire argument. He was not rejecting the nationalist cause because he disagreed with it politically. He was choosing a higher loyalty—the loyalty of love over the loyalty of wealth, the demands of family over the attractions of public acclaim.

In the course of his address, Jesus made several veiled references to his 'life mission,' though he did not elaborate. He suggested that this mission, whatever it might be, was inconsistent with the military path being proposed. But even this mission, he said, had been set aside in order to fulfill his obligation to his family.

Everyone in Nazareth knew Jesus was a devoted father to his siblings. This was a matter close to the heart of every respectable Jew. His appeal resonated deeply. Many who had been pressing him to join now felt ashamed of their pressure. They had been asking him to abandon the very qualities they most admired in him.

Still, some remained unconvinced. The situation might have deteriorated further if not for an unexpected intervention.

James stepped forward.

He was only thirteen years old, but he delivered a speech that had clearly been prepared in advance—coached, perhaps, by the chazan himself. James stated that he was certain Jesus would help liberate the Jewish people, but only when the time was right. If they would allow Jesus to remain as father and teacher to the family, they would eventually have not just one leader from Joseph's household, but five loyal nationalists. "Are there not five of us boys," James asked, "to grow up and come forth from our brother-father's guidance to serve our nation?"

It was brilliant rhetoric. James was offering a delayed but multiplied return on their investment. Let Jesus fulfill his family duty now, and in a few years, they would have five leaders instead of one.

The tension broke. The crowd, moved by the boy's earnestness and the obvious devotion between the brothers, accepted the explanation. The crisis passed.

But it left scars.

For several years afterward, there would be a coolness between Jesus and his uncle Simon. The town would remain divided in subtle ways. And Jesus himself had learned something crucial about the difficulty of his mission: he would always be caught between what people expected and what he actually was. He would always face pressure to fulfill roles that were not his to fill. He would always have to navigate between honesty and discretion, between revelation and restraint.

He had handled this crisis with remarkable skill for a seventeen-year-old. He had preserved his family obligations, maintained his integrity, and avoided open conflict with the nationalist movement. But the experience taught him that his path would not be simple. The world wanted a particular kind of Messiah—a political liberator, a military leader, a restorer of national glory.

That was not who he was.

What he was, he still could not fully articulate. But he knew with increasing certainty that his mission involved something deeper than politics, something more fundamental than national liberation, something that touched the very nature of God and man.

He would need more years to understand it fully. More years of ordinary work, ordinary struggle, ordinary human experience. More years of being a father to his siblings, a son to his mother, a carpenter in Nazareth.

The time for public revelation had not yet come. His hour had not yet arrived.

But it was coming. And when it did, the world would discover that the young man who knew God knew Him in ways no one had imagined possible.[1]

8

REBECCA

BY HIS EIGHTEENTH YEAR, THE NAZARETH FAMILY HAD BEEN STRIPPED OF nearly everything except the house itself and the small garden plot. The last pieces of property in Capernaum were sold, the proceeds used for taxes, new tools for James, and a down payment on the old family repair shop near the caravan lot. Jesus had arranged to buy back this shop—a strategic move that would allow him to meet travelers from across the region while James managed the house workshop.

With finances temporarily stabilized, Jesus made a decision that surprised Mary: he would take James to Jerusalem for Passover. The boy was now old enough to be received as a son of the commandment, and Jesus wanted to share with his brother the journey their father had once shared with him.

They traveled on foot through Samaria, Jesus pointing out the historic sites along the route just as Joseph had done five years earlier. James was religious by temperament, and though he didn't fully understand the plans surrounding his eldest brother's life, he looked forward to the day when he could assume full responsibility for the family and free Jesus for whatever mission awaited him. They talked more openly on this journey than ever before, discussing family matters and the future with a frankness that marked James's transition from boy to young man.

At Jerusalem, Jesus took James to Bethany for the Passover meal. Simon, their former host, had died and been laid to rest with his fathers. Jesus presided over the Passover as head of the family, having brought the lamb from the temple. After the meal, his mother sat with James while Jesus talked late into the night with Martha, Lazarus, and Mary.

The next day, James was received into the commonwealth of Israel. Standing on the brow of Olivet overlooking the temple, James exclaimed in wonder at the magnificent structure. Jesus stood beside him in silence, gazing at Jerusalem with an expression his brother could not interpret. There was something in that silence—something profound and sorrowful—that James could not understand.

James wanted to hear the temple teachers, hoping secretly to hear Jesus participate in the discussions as their mother had described from years before. But when they returned to hear the debates, Jesus asked no questions. The discussions seemed trivial to him now, these learned men arguing over minutiae while missing entirely the nature of the Father they claimed to serve. He could only pity them.

James was disappointed. To his inquiries, Jesus only replied: "My hour has not yet come."

They returned home through the Jordan valley, Jesus recounting memories of his earlier journey at age thirteen. Back in Nazareth, he began work in the family repair shop, cheered by the opportunity to meet people from all regions who stopped for repairs. Jesus loved people—common, ordinary people—and the shop became a gathering place for conversation and connection.

But the reprieve from hardship was brief. In December, death struck the family for the second time. Little Amos, the baby brother, died after a week of high fever. For four years their standard of living had steadily declined, and the funeral expenses on top of everything else nearly broke them.

Mary, grieving and anxious, looked to Jesus. He met her worry with practical optimism: "Mother-Mary, sorrow will not help us; we are all doing our best, and mother's smile might even inspire us to do better. Day by day we are strengthened for these tasks by our hope of better days ahead."

His sturdy faith was contagious. Despite grinding poverty, the household lived in an atmosphere of anticipation. The children developed strong and noble characters, sustained by Jesus's unwavering conviction that better days were coming.

By his nineteenth year, the household had found its rhythm. Jesus and Mary had reached a new understanding. She regarded him less as a son now and more as a father to her children. They spoke less frequently about his life's work, their conversations focused instead on the practical needs of raising four boys and three girls.

Jesus had revolutionized the family's approach to discipline, winning Mary over to his method of positive instruction rather than prohibition. He never said "thou shalt not"; instead, he commanded good: "You shall do this—you ought to do that." The children responded with prompt obedience, requiring little punishment. Only Jude, the firebrand of the family, occasionally needed correction for deliberate violations of household rules.

James was growing into a well-balanced youth, though less spiritually inclined than Jesus. Joseph was a faithful worker but a plodder, not reaching the intellectual level of his siblings. Simon was well-meaning but too much a dreamer, slow to settle down and a source of anxiety to both Jesus and Mary. Jude had the highest ideals but an unstable temperament—all his mother's determination without her sense of proportion.

Among the girls, Miriam was level-headed with a keen appreciation for noble things. Martha was slow but dependable. And little Ruth was the sunshine of the home, sincere of heart and beautiful, though not quite so lovely as Miriam, who was becoming the belle of Nazareth.

This was the year Jude started school. To pay the expenses, Jesus sold his harp—the last of his recreational pleasures. He had loved to play when tired in mind and weary in body, but he comforted himself that at least the instrument was safe from seizure by tax collectors.

The loss of the harp marked something deeper. Jesus was now twenty years old, and every dimension of personal enjoyment had been sacrificed to family necessity. He had no time for music, no opportunity for the philosophical discussions he craved, no space for the contemplation that fed his soul. He was carpenter, father, provider, teacher—everything except what he was meant to become.

And then Rebecca discovered she was in love with him.

Rebecca was the eldest daughter of Ezra, one of Nazareth's wealthiest merchants. She was beautiful, accomplished, from a family of means and social standing. Despite Jesus's poverty, his social position in Nazareth remained strong. He was regarded as one of the foremost young men of the city, admired by the young women for his physical strength, intellectual depth, and reputation as a spiritual leader.

It was not strange, then, that Rebecca should slowly fall in love with this son of Joseph. What was remarkable was what she chose to do about it.

She confided first in Miriam, Jesus's sister. Miriam, alarmed, went immediately to Mary. The news sent Mary into a spiral of conflicting emotions. Was she about to lose her son—the indispensable head of the family? Would troubles never cease? But beneath the practical anxiety lay another concern: what effect would marriage have on Jesus's future career? She had not forgotten—could never forget—that he was a child of promise.

Mary and Miriam decided to stop the situation before Jesus learned of it. They went to Rebecca directly and laid everything before her. They told her honestly what they believed: that Jesus was a son of destiny, destined to become a great religious leader, perhaps even the Messiah.

The revelation had the opposite effect of what they intended.

Rebecca listened, thrilled. She became more determined than ever to cast her lot with this man. She reasoned to herself that such a man would need a faithful and efficient wife all the more. She interpreted Mary's efforts as natural dread of losing the family's sole support. But she had a solution: her father would gladly provide sufficient income to compensate for the loss of Jesus's earnings.

When her father Ezra agreed to the plan, Rebecca had further conferences with Mary and Miriam. Meeting continued resistance, she made a bold decision: she would go directly to Jesus himself.

With her father's cooperation, she invited Jesus to their home for the celebration of her seventeenth birthday.

Jesus listened attentively as Ezra laid out the proposal. Then Rebecca herself spoke, explaining her feelings with the earnest clarity of first love. She was offering him everything: her devotion, her father's financial support for his family, freedom from the burden he had carried for six years.

Jesus listened with profound sympathy. When they finished, he made his reply with characteristic gentleness.

No amount of money, he said, could take the place of his obligation personally to rear his father's family—to fulfill "the most sacred of all human trusts: loyalty to one's own flesh and blood."

Ezra was deeply moved. He retired from the conference with a single remark to his wife: "We can't have him for a son; he is too noble for us."

Then Jesus spoke alone with Rebecca.

He thanked her sincerely for her expressed admiration, telling her it would cheer and comfort him all the days of his life. But he explained that he was not free to enter into relations with any woman beyond simple brotherly regard and pure friendship. His first and paramount duty was raising his father's family. He could not consider marriage until that was accomplished.

Then he said something that revealed the depth of his inner struggle: "If I am a son of destiny, I must not assume obligations of lifelong duration until such a time as my destiny shall be made manifest."

It was the most honest answer he could give. He did not yet fully understand his own mission, but he knew with certainty that it precluded the normal path of marriage and family. He was asking Rebecca to accept a refusal he could not fully explain even to himself.

Rebecca was heartbroken. She refused comfort. She begged her father to leave Nazareth, and eventually Ezra consented to move the family to Sepphoris.

But Rebecca never forgot. In the years that followed, many men sought her hand in marriage. To all of them, she had the same answer: no. She lived for one purpose—to await the hour when this man, the greatest who ever lived, would begin his career as a teacher of living truth.

She followed him devotedly through his years of public ministry, always from a distance, never imposing, never seeking recognition. She was present, unobserved by Jesus, on the day he rode triumphantly into Jerusalem. And she stood among the other women beside Mary on that fateful afternoon when the Son of Man hung upon the cross—to her, as to countless worlds on high, "the one altogether lovely and the greatest among ten thousand."

The story of Rebecca's love became known throughout Nazareth and later in Capernaum. From that time forward, while many women loved Jesus devotedly, none again offered him personal affection of the romantic kind. Human affection for him took on a different quality—more worshipful, more adoring, less possessive.

Miriam, watching her brother forsake even the love of a beautiful maiden, came to idealize Jesus with a profound affection that was part father-love, part brother-love, and entirely faithful.

***

Jesus' mother, with uncharacteristic wisdom, suggested he make a journey to Jerusalem for Passover. He leaped at the opportunity. What he most wanted—though he was not fully conscious of it—was time with Lazarus, Martha, and Mary. Next to his own family, he loved these three most of all.

He traveled through Megiddo, Antipatris, and Lydda, spending four days on the journey, thinking much about the past. When he reached Jerusalem, he passed through quickly, pausing only to look at the temple and the crowds. He had developed a strange aversion to this Herod-built temple with its politically appointed priesthood. His destination was Bethany.

Lazarus was now the same age Jesus had been when Joseph died— barely fourteen—and had recently become head of his own household after his mother's death. Martha was a year older than Jesus, and Mary was two years younger. Jesus was the idolized ideal of all three.

The visit was exactly what Jesus needed. Here, among people who loved him without expectation or demand, he could simply be himself. They talked late into the nights. They shared meals. They laughed. For a few precious days, Jesus was not the head of a belea- guered household or the object of someone's romantic devotion or the mysterious young man who knew God. He was simply a friend, visiting friends, resting his soul.

When he returned to Nazareth, he was ready to resume the work. The years ahead would bring more challenges, more sacrifices, more tests of his resolve. But he had learned something essential from the Rebecca experience: his path would require renunciations that ordinary people would find incomprehensible. He would be asked to give up not only the comfort of wealth and the attractions of power, but also the deepest human consolations—the love of a wife, the joy of children, the ordinary satisfactions of domestic life.

He had chosen the harder path. Not because human love was wrong, but because his mission required a different kind of devotion. Rebecca had offered him everything a man could want. He had refused it all because something greater was calling—something he could barely articulate but could not deny.

Someday the world would understand why. Someday his mission would be revealed. Someday people would comprehend what it meant to be a son of destiny.

But not yet. His hour had not yet come.

For now, there was only the work—the endless, grinding, glorious work of being a father to his brothers and sisters, a comfort to his mother, and a faithful steward of the trust his father Joseph had left in his hands.[1]

9

———

THE FAMILY YEARS

At twenty-one, Jesus entered upon the task he had been born to accomplish with full self-consciousness and unwavering purpose. He understood now, more clearly than ever, the twofold nature of his existence: he was Joshua ben Joseph, son of a Nazareth carpenter, and simultaneously something far greater—a being whose ultimate mission would shake the foundations of human understanding. He was learning how to effectively combine these two natures into one unified personality, but the integration was not without difficulty. How does God learn to be human? How does divinity submit to the limitations of mortality?

The answer, Jesus had discovered, was through experience—genuine, unmitigated human experience. And so he continued his preparation, year by patient year, living as completely as possible the life of an ordinary man.

This year he took Joseph, his younger brother, to Jerusalem for Passover. Just as he had once journeyed with James, he now shared this formative experience with the next son in line. They traveled the Jordan valley route, Jesus narrating Jewish history as they walked. Joseph asked many leading questions about his eldest brother's life mission, curious about the destiny that everyone sensed but no one quite understood.

To most of these inquiries, Jesus would only reply: "My hour has not yet come."

But in those intimate discussions, walking the dusty roads between Nazareth and Jerusalem, Jesus dropped hints that Joseph would remember years later when the full revelation finally came. They celebrated Passover at Bethany with Lazarus, Martha, and Mary—Jesus's closest friends outside his own family. The time spent with these three always refreshed his soul in ways the Nazareth household could not.

By his twenty-second year, the family dynamic had shifted considerably. Jesus's brothers and sisters ranged from seven to eighteen years old, all facing the trials and tribulations of adolescence. Jesus helped them navigate the emotional awakening, the intellectual questioning, the social pressures. He had become expert at addressing the problems of young people transitioning into adulthood.

This was the year Simon graduated from synagogue school and began working with Jacob, the stone mason who had been Jesus's childhood playmate. The family had decided to diversify their trades. Not all the boys would be carpenters. By spreading across different crafts, they could eventually take contracts for entire buildings.

Jesus continued house finishing and cabinetwork, but increasingly he spent time at the caravan repair shop. James was beginning to alternate with him there, learning to manage both the business and the diverse clientele. Then, when carpenter work grew slack in Nazareth, Jesus made a strategic decision: he left James in charge of the repair shop and Joseph at the home workbench, and went to Sepphoris to work with a smith.

Before leaving, he held a family conference—one of those periodic gatherings where important decisions were formally acknowledged. With appropriate solemnity, Jesus installed James, now just past eighteen, as acting head of the family. He promised his brother full support and cooperation. He extracted formal promises of obedience to James from each family member.

From that day forward, James assumed financial responsibility for the household. Jesus continued working and contributing, but the ultimate authority had been transferred. Never again would Jesus take the reins back from James's hands.

The move to Sepphoris was deliberate. Jesus could have walked home every night—it was only four miles. But he purposely remained away, assigning weather and work as reasons, though his true motive was to train James and Joseph in bearing family responsibility alone. He was beginning the slow, careful process of weaning his family from dependence on his immediate presence.

He returned to Nazareth each Sabbath, and sometimes during the week when needed, to observe how the new arrangement was working. He offered advice. He made helpful suggestions. But he did not interfere with James's decisions.

Living in Sepphoris for six months gave Jesus opportunity to understand the gentile viewpoint more deeply. He worked with gentiles, lived among them, studied their habits and their way of thinking. The experience was valuable, but the moral standards of Herod Antipas's capital city were far below even those of the caravan city of Nazareth. When the opportunity came to return home, Jesus took it gladly.

But he did not resume personal direction of family affairs. He worked alongside James in the repair shop, but James continued managing the home and the budget. The plan was working. The family was learning to function without Jesus at the center.

By his twenty-third year, financial pressure had eased. Four family members were working. Miriam earned considerable money selling milk and butter. Martha had become an expert weaver. The repair shop was more than one-third paid off. For the first time since Joseph's death, the household breathed easy.

Jesus decided to take Simon to Jerusalem for Passover—the first extended time away from daily work since his father died nine years earlier. They journeyed through the Decapolis, visiting Pella, Gerasa, Philadelphia, Heshbon, and Jericho. They returned by the coastal route, touching Lydda, Joppa, Caesarea, and around Mount Carmel to Ptolemais and home.

The trip acquainted Jesus thoroughly with Palestine north of Jerusalem. But more significantly, it brought two encounters that would have profound consequences years later.

At Philadelphia, they met a merchant from Damascus—a wealthy, well-educated man of world affairs who owned over four thousand caravan camels and had business interests throughout the Roman world. He developed an immediate liking for Jesus. The two talked for hours about philosophy, commerce, and the nature of God. The merchant proposed that Jesus come to Damascus to enter his Oriental import business.

Jesus explained that he could not justify going so far from his family just then. But on the journey home, he thought much about those distant cities the merchant had described—cities of the Far West and the Far East that caravan travelers spoke of with such enthusiasm.

In Jerusalem, while Simon attended Passover ceremonies, Jesus mingled with the crowds and engaged in numerous conversations with gentile visitors. The most notable was with a young Greek named Stephen. They met by chance on Thursday afternoon of Passover week and fell into a discussion that lasted four hours—a conversation about the way of life, the true God, and authentic worship.

Stephen was tremendously impressed. He never forgot Jesus's words. Fifteen years later, this same Stephen would become a believer in Jesus's teachings and would die for his boldness in preaching the early gospel—stoned to death by irate Jews who could not tolerate his attack on their temple and its traditions. Standing by as Stephen yielded up his life would be a man named Saul of Tarsus, and the sight of a Greek dying for his faith would plant seeds in Saul's heart that would eventually lead him to become Paul, the aggressive and indomitable architect of Christian theology.

But neither Stephen nor Jesus knew any of this that afternoon in Jerusalem. They were simply two young men talking about God.

The Damascus merchant had not forgotten Jesus. Later that year, a representative sought out Jesus in Nazareth and escorted him to Damascus for what would become one of the greatest temptations of his purely human career.

The merchant proposed to devote an extraordinary sum of money to establishing a school of religious philosophy that would rival Alexandria. He wanted Jesus to tour the world's educational centers as preparation for becoming the head of this new institution. It was a magnificent opportunity—exactly the kind of position that would have fulfilled every dream Mary had ever held for her son.

Jesus spent four months in Damascus as the merchant's guest. During this time, he met with a group of twelve merchants and bankers who agreed to fund the project. They pressed their case with passion and persistence. Here was a chance to become a renowned teacher, to influence thousands, to establish a center of learning that would endure for generations.

Jesus manifested deep interest in the proposed school. He helped them plan its organization. But he expressed concern about "other and unstated but prior obligations" that would prevent his accepting such a pretentious responsibility.

He knew that his mission could not be supported by institutions of learning. He knew he must not obligate himself to be directed by "the councils of men," no matter how well-intentioned. His would-be benefactor employed him at translation work while his family tried to change Jesus's mind.

But Jesus would not consent. The Damascus businessmen, disappointed but respectful, never connected the later teacher from Capernaum who turned Judea upside down with the obscure carpenter who had declined their generous offer.

Jesus returned to Nazareth and resumed his daily work as if nothing had happened. He never spoke of the Damascus episode to his family.

By his twenty-fourth year, Jesus enjoyed his first period of comparative freedom from grinding family responsibility. James had proven himself capable. The household ran smoothly. The children were growing up well.

Then came another temptation—this time from Alexandria.

A young man arrived in Nazareth to arrange a meeting between Jesus and prominent Alexandrian Jews. In June, Jesus traveled to Caesarea to meet with five distinguished men who offered him a position as assistant to the chazan in Alexandria's chief synagogue. They explained that Alexandria was destined to become the headquarters of Jewish culture for the entire world. They reminded him of the dangerous rebellion brewing in Jerusalem and predicted—with chilling accuracy—that any Palestinian uprising would be crushed by Rome within three months, that Jerusalem would be destroyed, the temple demolished.

They offered Jesus escape from this coming catastrophe and the opportunity to become a great teacher in the most influential Jewish city in the world.

Jesus listened to everything they said. He thanked them for their confidence. Then he declined: "My hour has not yet come."

They were astonished by his apparent indifference to such an honor. They presented him with a purse of money in token of esteem and compensation for his travel. Jesus refused that too: "The house of Joseph has never received alms, and we cannot eat another's bread as long as I have strong arms and my brothers can labor."

The Alexandrian delegation sailed home, bewildered. Years later, when they heard rumors of a Capernaum boatbuilder creating a commotion in Palestine, few of them connected him with the strange Galilean who had so mysteriously declined their invitation.

Jesus returned to Nazareth and enjoyed six months of unusual peace. He communed much with his Father in heaven and made tremendous progress in mastering his human mind.

But human affairs never run smoothly for long. In December, James came to Jesus with private news: he was deeply in love with Esta, a young woman of Nazareth, and wanted permission to marry.

Jesus gave his consent—but set the wedding date two years in the future. During that time, James would properly train Joseph to assume direction of the home. The machinery of Jesus's departure from family life was advancing another step.

Soon Miriam approached with similar news. Jacob the stone mason, Jesus's old childhood friend and defender, had long sought Miriam's hand. Jesus promised his blessing for the marriage as soon as Martha was competent to assume Miriam's household duties.

Marriage was in the air. The children were growing up. The family was moving toward the future. And Jesus's time of release was drawing closer.

<hr>

His twenty-fifth year began with the entire Nazareth family in good health. The regular schooling of all the children was complete except for some work Martha needed to do with Ruth. The family finances were better than they had been since Joseph's death. Final payments had been made on the repair shop. For the first time in years, they owed no one and had some money saved.

Jesus decided to take Jude to Jerusalem for his first Passover. Jude had just graduated from synagogue school and was ready to join the congregation of Israel. They traveled by the Jordan valley route— Jesus feared trouble if he took his impulsive young brother through Samaria.

They arrived in Jerusalem and were making their first visit to the temple when they encountered Lazarus of Bethany. While Jesus talked with his friend about celebrating Passover together, Jude started real trouble.

A Roman guard made improper remarks about a passing Jewish girl. Jude flushed with indignation and expressed his resentment directly to the soldier. Roman legionnaires were notoriously sensitive to Jewish disrespect. The guard promptly placed Jude under arrest.

Before Jesus could intervene, Jude had delivered a voluble denunciation of pent-up anti-Roman feelings. He was taken to military prison, and Jesus went with him.

Jesus tried to obtain immediate release or at least a hearing before Passover evening, but he failed. The next day was a holy convocation —even Romans would not hear charges against a Jew on such a day. Jude remained in confinement two full days. Jesus stayed at the prison with him the entire time.

They missed the temple ceremony that would have inducted Jude into the state of Israel. The boy would have to postpone completing this rite of passage.

On the morning of the third day, Jesus appeared before the military magistrate. He apologized for his brother's youth. He explained, carefully but honestly, the provocative nature of the incident. He handled the case so skillfully that the magistrate expressed sympathy, suggesting that the young Jew might have had some excuse for his outburst.

The magistrate issued a warning to Jude, then turned to Jesus with prophetic words: "You had better keep your eye on the lad; he's liable to make a lot of trouble for all of you."

The Roman judge spoke the truth. Jude would make considerable trouble for Jesus in years to come—always clashes with civil authorities due to thoughtless patriotic outbursts.

They walked to Bethany that night, explaining their absence to Lazarus and his sisters, and returned to Nazareth the following day. Jesus had a long talk with Jude about the episode three weeks later. The young man never forgot the patience and forbearance his brother-father showed throughout that ordeal.

This was the last Passover Jesus would attend with any member of his own family. Increasingly, the Son of Man was becoming separated from close association with his own flesh and blood.

Yet that year, his seasons of deep meditation were constantly interrupted by Ruth and her playmates. Jesus was always ready to postpone contemplation of his future work to share in childlike joy and youthful gladness. The children never tired of his stories about Jerusalem, about animals, about nature.

They loved coming to the repair shop. Jesus provided sand, blocks, and stones beside the workshop, and children flocked there to play. When they tired of play, the boldest would peek inside. If Jesus wasn't busy, they would venture in and say, "Uncle Joshua, come out and tell us a big story."

They would lead him out by his hands to the favorite rock by the corner of the shop. The children would sit on the ground in a semicircle before him—sometimes the smallest climbing onto his knees— looking up in wonder at his expressive face as he told his stories.

The children loved Jesus. And Jesus loved the children. He taught them to laugh, and to laugh heartily.

It was difficult for his friends to comprehend the range of his intellectual activities—how he could swing so suddenly from profound discussions of politics, philosophy, or religion to the lighthearted playfulness of children. But Jesus saw no contradiction. The kingdom he would eventually proclaim belonged especially to children—children of God.

His twenty-sixth year began with Jesus strongly conscious that he possessed a wide range of potential power. But he was equally persuaded that this power must not be employed by his personality as the Son of Man—at least not until his hour came.

He thought much but said little about his relationship with his Father in heaven. The conclusion of all his thinking was expressed once in prayer on the hilltop: "Regardless of who I am and what power I may or may not wield, I always have been, and always will be, subject to the will of my Paradise Father."

The family affairs ran smoothly this year, with one exception: Jude. The youngest brother was not inclined to settle down to regular work, nor could he be depended upon for his share of home expenses. James and Joseph favored casting him out. Jesus would not consent. When their patience wore thin, he would say: "Be patient. Be wise in your counsel and eloquent in your lives, that your young brother may first know the better way and then be constrained to follow you in it."

The wise and loving counsel prevented a family rupture. But Jude would not come to his sober senses until after his marriage—still years away.

Mary seldom spoke anymore of Jesus's future mission. When the subject arose, Jesus only replied: "My hour has not yet come." She had almost given up trying to understand her firstborn son. She sensed he was preparing to leave them, but she could not comprehend where he would go or what he would do.

Jesus afforded unusual time this year to individual family members. He took them on long strolls through the countryside. He brought Jude to a farmer uncle south of Nazareth, though the boy ran away before harvest and had to be retrieved from the fishermen at the lake. Jesus arranged for Jude to work with a relative in Magdala, and there the volatile young man finally found his calling.

At last, all of Jesus's brothers had chosen their lifework. The stage was set for his departure.

In November, the day finally arrived. James and Esta, Miriam and Jacob—a double wedding. It was a joyous occasion. Even Mary found herself happy, though every now and then she realized with fresh pain that Jesus was preparing to leave. She suffered under a great uncertainty, wishing he would sit down and talk freely as he had when he was a boy. But Jesus remained profoundly silent about the future.

James and Esta moved into a small home on the west side of town, a gift from her father. James continued supporting his mother's household, though his contribution was cut in half now that he had his own family. Joseph was formally installed by Jesus as head of the family finances. Jude, working steadily now as a fisherman, faithfully sent his share home each month. The weddings had a beneficial influence on the young man.

Miriam moved next door to Mary, into Jacob's family home. Martha took Miriam's place in the household. The new organization worked smoothly before the year ended.

The day after the double wedding, Jesus held an important conference with James. He spoke confidentially, telling his brother that he was preparing to leave home. Then, with formal solemnity, Jesus presented full title to the repair shop to James and most touchingly established him as "head and protector of my father's house."

They drew up and signed a secret compact. In return for the gift of the repair shop, James would assume full financial responsibility for the family, releasing Jesus from all further obligations. Jesus would continue sending money each month until his hour came, but those funds would be applied by James as he saw fit—for family necessities, pleasures, sickness, or unexpected emergencies.

It was done. After fifteen years, Jesus had successfully prepared his family to function without him.

He had raised his brothers and sisters. He had trained his successor. He had secured the family's financial future. He had fulfilled every obligation to his father's household.

Now, at last, he was ready to enter upon the second phase of his adult life—the phase detached from home, moving toward his Father's business.

His hour had not yet come. But it was coming soon.

And when it arrived, the family he had so faithfully nurtured would watch in bewilderment as their carpenter brother transformed into something no one had anticipated—a teacher whose words would echo through eternity, revealing the Father in heaven in ways that would forever change humanity's understanding of God.

But that day lay ahead. For now, there was only the quiet satisfaction of work completed, duty fulfilled, and a family standing strong.

Jesus had prepared them to let him go. The question remaining was whether they—especially Mary—would ever be able to understand why he had to leave.[1]

10

THE BOATBUILDER

On a rainy Sunday morning in January, Jesus left Nazareth. There was no ceremony, no formal farewell gathering. He simply explained to his family that he was going to Tiberias and then would visit other cities around the Sea of Galilee. He embraced his mother, said goodbye to his brothers and sisters, and walked out into the rain.

He would never again be a regular member of that household.

For more than four years, the family had sensed this day was coming. Jesus had gradually prepared them, step by careful step, for his eventual departure. The sadness they felt was tempered by this long preparation, but Mary's heart still broke as she watched her firstborn son walk away down the muddy road toward an unknown future.

Jesus had made every preparation for this permanent separation, and it had not been easy. He naturally loved his people. His affection for his family had been tremendously augmented by his extraordinary devotion to them over fifteen years. The more fully we give ourselves to others, the more we come to love them—and Jesus had given himself completely to this family. He loved them with a great and fervent affection.

His training as a man of the realm was nearly complete. Soon he would enter upon his public ministry. First, however, he needed these final years of freedom and diverse experience.

He spent one week in Tiberias, the new city that was replacing Sepphoris as Galilee's capital. Finding little to interest him there, he moved on through Magdala and Bethsaida to Capernaum, where he stopped to visit his father's old friend Zebedee.

Zebedee's sons—James, John, and David—were fishermen. Zebedee himself was a boatbuilder. Jesus of Nazareth was an expert in both designing and building; he was a master at working with wood. Zebedee had long known of the Nazareth craftsman's skill. For some time now, he had been contemplating making improved boats. When Jesus arrived, Zebedee laid his plans before him and invited the visiting carpenter to join the enterprise.

Jesus readily consented.

What followed was one of the most settled and productive periods of Jesus's entire life. He worked with Zebedee for slightly more than a year, and during that time he revolutionized boatbuilding on the Sea of Galilee.

Jesus created an entirely new style of boat. Using superior technique and greatly improved methods of steaming boards, he and Zebedee began producing craft of a very superior type—vessels far safer for sailing the lake than the older designs. The boats were sturdier, more maneuverable, more seaworthy. Within five years, practically every craft on the lake had been built in Zebedee's shop at Capernaum using Jesus's designs.

Jesus became well known to the Galilean fisherfolk as the designer of the new boats. It was work he loved—creative, practical, immediately useful. He was solving real problems, making life safer and easier for working men. The satisfaction was deep and genuine.

Zebedee was a moderately prosperous man. His boatbuilding shops sat on the lakeshore south of Capernaum, and his home was situated down the shore near the fishing headquarters of Bethsaida. Jesus lived in Zebedee's home throughout the year, and he greatly enjoyed this period of working with a father-partner. He had worked alone in the world for so long—without a father—that the companionship with Zebedee filled a void he had scarcely recognized.

Zebedee's wife, Salome, was a relative of Annas, the former high priest at Jerusalem. Though Annas had been deposed eight years earlier, he remained the most influential figure among the Sadducees. Salome became a great admirer of Jesus. She loved him as she loved her own sons, and her four daughters regarded Jesus as their elder brother.

Jesus often went fishing with James, John, and David. They discovered he was as experienced a fisherman as he was an expert boatbuilder. The Zebedee family came to almost worship him. They never missed the question-and-answer sessions he conducted each evening after supper, before departing for the synagogue to study. Young neighbors also attended these gatherings, where Jesus offered varied and advanced instruction on politics, sociology, science, and philosophy—always adapted to what his audience could comprehend.

He talked freely about these subjects but never presumed to speak with authoritative finality except when discussing religion—the relationship between man and God. On that subject, his certainty was absolute.

Once a week Jesus held meetings with all of Zebedee's employees—household staff, shop workers, and shore helpers. It was among these workers that Jesus was first called "the Master." They all loved him. Of Zebedee's sons, James was most interested in Jesus as a philosopher; John cared most for his religious teaching; David respected him as a mechanic but took little interest in his spiritual views.

Throughout this year, Jesus sent money each month to James in

Nazareth. He returned home once, in October, to attend Martha's wedding, and then was not in Nazareth again for over two years.

He continued observing how men lived on earth. Capernaum was on the direct travel route from Damascus southward, and Jesus frequently visited the caravan station, talking with travelers from distant lands. The city was also a strong Roman military post. The garrison commander was a gentile believer in Yahweh—"a devout man," as Jews called such proselytes. This officer had built a beautiful synagogue in Capernaum and presented it to the Jewish community.

Jesus conducted services in this new synagogue more than half the time during his year in Capernaum. Caravan travelers who attended occasionally remembered him as "the carpenter from Nazareth."

When it came time to pay taxes, Jesus registered himself as a "skilled craftsman of Capernaum." From that day forward, to the end of his earthly life, he was legally a resident of Capernaum. He never claimed any other legal residence, though others would later assign him to Damascus, Bethany, Nazareth, or even Alexandria.

At the Capernaum synagogue, Jesus found many new books in the library chests. He spent at least five evenings a week in intense study. One evening he devoted to social life with older folks, and one evening he spent with young people. There was something gracious and inspiring about his personality that invariably attracted youth. He always made them feel at ease. His secret, perhaps, lay in the twofold fact that he was genuinely interested in what they were doing, and he seldom offered advice unless they asked for it.

This year Jesus made great advances in the mastery of his human mind and attained new and high levels of conscious communion with his Father in heaven. The spiritual progress was profound, though invisible to those around him.

This was the last year of his settled life. Never again would Jesus spend a whole year in one place or at one undertaking. The days of his earth pilgrimages were rapidly approaching. Periods of intense activity were not far in the future. But first, there would intervene a few years of extensive travel and highly diversified personal activity. He had more to learn before that momentous day wherein he would enter upon his career as teacher and revealer of the Father.

Frequently, Jude came over from his fishing work on the Sabbath to hear Jesus speak in the synagogue and would stay to visit. The more Jude saw of his eldest brother, the more convinced he became that Jesus was truly a great man—though he still couldn't fathom exactly what kind of greatness his brother embodied.

In March of the following year, Jesus took leave of Zebedee and Capernaum. He asked for a small sum of money to cover his expenses to Jerusalem. During his time with Zebedee, he had drawn only modest wages, sending most of it monthly to Nazareth. One month Joseph would come to Capernaum for the money; the next month Jude would come over and take it home.

Before leaving, Jesus had a long, private conversation with John Zebedee—his new-found friend and close companion. Jesus told John he contemplated traveling extensively "until my hour shall come." He asked John to act in his place, sending money to the Nazareth family each month until the funds due him were exhausted.

John's promise was immediate and wholehearted: "My Teacher, go about your business, do your work in the world. I will act for you in this or any other matter. I will watch over your family even as I would foster my own mother and care for my own brothers and sisters. I will disburse your funds which my father holds as you have directed. And when your money has been expended, if I do not receive more from you, and if your mother is in need, then I will share my own earnings with her. Go your way in peace. I will act in your stead in all these matters."

After Jesus departed for Jerusalem, John consulted with his father about the money due Jesus. He was surprised to discover it was a substantial sum. They agreed it would be wiser to invest the funds in property and use the income to assist the Nazareth family. Zebedee knew of a small two-room house in Capernaum that carried a mortgage and was for sale. He directed John to buy the house with Jesus's money and hold the title in trust for his friend.

For two years, the rent from this house was applied to the mortgage. This, combined with a large sum Jesus would later send to John from abroad, nearly paid off the obligation. Zebedee supplied the difference, and John secured clear title. Jesus became the owner of a house in Capernaum—though no one ever told him about it.

When the Nazareth family learned Jesus had left Capernaum, they assumed—not knowing of the financial arrangement with John—that the time had come to manage without further help. James remembered his contract with Jesus and, with his brothers' help, assumed full responsibility for the family's support.

Jesus spent almost two months in Jerusalem, devoting most of his time to listening to temple discussions and visiting the various schools of the rabbis. Most Sabbaths he spent at Bethany with Lazarus, Martha, and Mary.

He carried with him a letter from Salome introducing him to Annas, the former high priest, as "one, the same as my own son." Annas spent considerable time with Jesus, personally taking him to visit the many academies of Jerusalem's religious teachers. Jesus thoroughly inspected these schools and carefully observed their teaching methods, but he never asked a single public question.

Annas regarded Jesus as a great man but was puzzled about how to advise him. He recognized the foolishness of suggesting Jesus enter any Jerusalem school as a student, yet he knew Jesus would never be accorded the status of a regular teacher since he had no formal training. It was an impasse. Here was an obvious genius with no credentials, in a world where credentials were everything.

Before Passover week ended, Jesus met a wealthy traveler from India and his seventeen-year-old son. These travelers were on their way to Rome and various Mediterranean points, and they had arranged to arrive in Jerusalem during Passover hoping to find someone to serve as both interpreter and tutor for the son.

The father was insistent that Jesus consent to travel with them. When Jesus mentioned his family obligations, the merchant proposed to advance one year's wages so Jesus could provide for his family's needs during his absence. It was an extraordinary offer—the opportunity to see the Roman world, to meet diverse peoples, to experience cultures Jesus had only heard about from caravan travelers.

Jesus agreed to make the trip.

He turned the large advance payment over to John Zebedee, who would apply it toward the house mortgage and use the remainder for family support. Jesus took Zebedee fully into his confidence about the Mediterranean journey but enjoined him to tell no one—not even his own family. Zebedee never disclosed his knowledge of Jesus's whereabouts during the nearly two years that followed.

As months passed with no word from Jesus, the Nazareth family gradually gave him up as dead. Only the assurances of Zebedee, who went to Nazareth with his son John on several occasions, kept hope alive in Mary's heart.

The family managed well in Jesus's absence. Jude had considerably increased his contribution and kept up the extra amount even after he married. John Zebedee faithfully brought funds each month to Mary and Ruth, as promised.

Jesus's entire twenty-ninth year was spent touring the Mediterranean world. For many reasons—primarily to avoid drawing attention to himself—he was known throughout most of this journey as "the

Damascus scribe." At Corinth and other stops on the return trip, he was called "the Jewish tutor."

This was an eventful period. Jesus made contact with hundreds of his fellow human beings during these travels, but this experience remained a phase of his life he never revealed to any member of his family or to any of his apostles. Only Zebedee of Bethsaida knew the facts, and Zebedee told no one.

Some of Jesus's friends thought he had returned to Damascus. Others believed he had gone to India. His own family inclined toward the belief that he was in Alexandria, since they knew he had once been invited there. When Jesus eventually returned to Palestine, he did nothing to change their opinion. He permitted them to continue believing he had spent those years in Alexandria.

The real purpose of the Mediterranean journey was simple: to know men. Jesus came close to hundreds of people on this trip. He met and loved all manner of humanity. He learned how they lived, what they believed, what they feared, what they hoped for. He ate their food, learned their customs, spoke their languages. He worked alongside them, laughed with them, mourned with them. He became, in the deepest sense, familiar with the entire range of human experience across the diverse cultures of the Roman world.

On this journey, Jesus made great advances in his human task of mastering the material and mortal mind. His divine nature made corresponding progress in the spiritual understanding of that same human intellect. By the end of this tour, Jesus virtually knew—with all human certainty—that he was a Son of God.

The divine spirit within him was increasingly able to bring up in Jesus's consciousness memories of his existence before his earthly birth—memories from his prior estate in the heavenly realms. Little by little, these impressions of his former existence in the epochs of the eternal past came to the surface.

The last memory to emerge was from just before he surrendered his divine consciousness to embark upon his earthly incarnation. This final memory picture would be made clear in Jesus's consciousness on the very day of his baptism by John in the Jordan.

The purely human religious experience—the personal spiritual growth—of the Son of Man reached near its apex during this twenty-ninth year. The spiritual development had been consistently gradual from his earliest years until now, when the natural relationship between his material human mind and indwelling divine spirit approached completion.

Jesus experienced the wide range of human emotion during these travels—from superb joy to profound sorrow. He was a child of joy and a being of rare good humor, yet he was also intimately acquainted with grief. He lived through every usual and familiar period of human intellectual and spiritual advancement, and he also fully experienced those higher phases of divine-human unity that so few mortals ever attain.

To the celestial intelligences watching from throughout the universe, this Mediterranean journey was the most enthralling of all Jesus's earth experiences up to that time.

He was the carpenter of Nazareth, the boatbuilder of Capernaum, the scribe of Damascus. He was the Son of Man, not yet having achieved complete unification of his human consciousness with his divine nature. He was a man among men, and he was completing the experience of living the full life of a human creature.

By the end of his twenty-ninth year, Jesus of Nazareth had virtually finished living the life required of a mortal sojourner in the flesh. He came to earth as the fullness of God to be manifest to man. He had now become nearly the perfection of man awaiting the occasion to become manifest to God. And he accomplished all of this before he was thirty years of age.[1]

11

THE DAMASCUS SCRIBE

They left Jerusalem on a Sunday morning in late April—Jesus and two travelers from India, a wealthy merchant named Gonod and his seventeen-year-old son Ganid. The arrangement was straightforward: Jesus would serve as interpreter and tutor during their tour of the Roman world. In return, he would receive wages sufficient to support his family in Nazareth during his absence.

For the next year and eight months, these three men would travel together across the Mediterranean—from Jerusalem to Caesarea, Alexandria, Carthage, Rome, Athens, and eventually to the Persian Gulf where Gonod and Ganid would embark for India while Jesus returned to Palestine. It would be one of the most extraordinary journeys in human history, though no one at the time recognized it as such.

Throughout this tour, Jesus was known by various names depending on the city. Most commonly, he was called "the Damascus scribe"—a reference to the four months he had spent in Damascus before this journey, where he had learned the rudiments of Gonod's language. At Corinth and other stops on the return trip, he would be known as "the Jewish tutor."

No one suspected that this quiet interpreter was anything other than what he appeared to be: a skilled craftsman and translator helping a wealthy merchant navigate the complexities of Mediterranean commerce and culture.

Jesus spent roughly half of each day teaching Ganid and interpreting during Gonod's business conferences and social contacts. The remainder of his time—which was at his disposal—he devoted to something Ganid found increasingly fascinating: making personal contacts with ordinary people.

It was a pattern of behavior that would characterize these years leading up to his public ministry. Jesus sought out people—not crowds, not audiences, but individuals. He talked with them, listened to their problems, understood their struggles, and offered wisdom that addressed their specific circumstances.

Ganid watched this with growing curiosity. Why did his tutor occupy himself so continuously with visits to strangers? What motivated these incessant activities?

The answer would gradually become clear over the course of their journey. Jesus was engaged in a kind of ministry—personal, private, utterly focused on individual human beings and their genuine needs. He was learning humanity one person at a time, and simultaneously helping each person he encountered to know God more fully.

Their first significant stop was Joppa, the ancient port city on the Mediterranean coast. While Gonod conducted business with a local tanner named Simon, Jesus met a young Philistine interpreter named Gadiah who worked for Simon.

Gadiah was a truth seeker. Jesus was a truth giver.

One evening after supper, Jesus and Gadiah strolled down by the sea. Gadiah, not knowing that this Damascus scribe was deeply versed in Hebrew traditions, pointed out the ship landing from which Jonah was reputed to have embarked on his ill-fated voyage to Tarshish.

"But do you suppose," Gadiah asked with genuine curiosity, "the big fish really did swallow Jonah?"

Jesus perceived immediately that this young man's life had been tremendously influenced by the Jonah story, and that contemplating it had impressed upon him the folly of running away from duty. Rather than destroy the foundations of Gadiah's present motivation for practical living, Jesus responded with a parable.

"My friend, we are all Jonahs with lives to live in accordance with the will of God. And whenever we seek to escape the present duty of living by running away to far-off enticements, we put ourselves in the control of influences not directed by truth and righteousness. The flight from duty is the sacrifice of truth. The escape from the service of light and life can only result in those distressing conflicts with the difficult whales of selfishness which lead eventually to darkness and death—unless such God-forsaking Jonahs turn their hearts, even when in the very depths of despair, to seek after God and his goodness."

He paused, watching the young man's face in the fading light. "And when such disheartened souls sincerely seek for God—hunger for truth and thirst for righteousness—there is nothing that can hold them in further captivity. No matter into what great depths they may have fallen, when they seek the light with a whole heart, the spirit of the Lord God of heaven will deliver them from their captivity. The evil circumstances of life will spew them out upon the dry land of fresh opportunities for renewed service and wiser living."

Gadiah was profoundly moved. They talked long into the night by the seaside, and before they returned to their lodgings, they prayed together and for each other.

This same Gadiah would later listen to Peter's preaching and become a profound believer in Jesus of Nazareth. He would hold a memorable argument with Peter one evening at the home of Dorcas. And Gadiah would have much to do with the final decision of Simon the wealthy leather merchant to embrace the Christian faith.

But on this night, Gadiah was simply a young man talking with a stranger by the sea, finding in that stranger's words something that resonated with the deepest yearnings of his soul.

Before they parted, Gadiah asked Jesus about the problem of evil. "How can God, if he is infinitely good, permit us to suffer the sorrows of evil? After all, who creates evil?"

Jesus's answer was clear and uncompromising. "My brother, God is love; therefore he must be good, and his goodness is so great and real that it cannot contain the small and unreal things of evil. God is so positively good that there is absolutely no place in him for negative evil."

He continued, his voice gentle but firm. "Evil is the immature choosing and the unthinking misstep of those who are resistant to goodness, rejectful of beauty, and disloyal to truth. Evil is only the misadaptation of immaturity or the disruptive influence of ignorance. Evil is the inevitable darkness which follows upon the heels of the unwise rejection of light. Evil is that which is dark and untrue, and which, when consciously embraced and willfully endorsed, becomes sin."

The distinction was crucial. Evil was not created by God. Evil emerged from the misuse of God-given freedom—the power to choose between truth and error, between light and darkness.

Gadiah understood. The conversation had made clear to his mind the real meaning of these momentous truths. God did not create evil. Humans created evil by choosing poorly. And humans could escape evil by choosing better.

From Joppa they traveled to Caesarea, intending to take a boat to Alexandria. But they were delayed when one of the huge steering paddles on their vessel was discovered to be dangerously cracked. The captain decided to remain in port while a replacement was made.

There was a shortage of skilled woodworkers for this task. Jesus, the master carpenter and boatbuilder, volunteered to assist.

During the days he spent working in the shipyard, Jesus encountered a young Greek named Anaxand who labored alongside him on the steering paddle. Anaxand became interested in the words Jesus dropped from hour to hour as they toiled together.

One day Jesus intimated that the Father in heaven was interested in the welfare of his children on earth. Anaxand was skeptical. "If the Gods are interested in me," he said bitterly, "then why do they not remove the cruel and unjust foreman of this workshop?"

Jesus stopped his work and looked at the young man. "Since you know the ways of kindness and value justice, perhaps the Gods have brought this erring man near so that you may lead him into a better way. Maybe you are the salt which is to make this brother more agreeable to all other men—that is, if you have not lost your savor."

Anaxand frowned, not understanding.

Jesus continued, his tone patient. "As it is, this man is your master in that his evil ways unfavorably influence you. Why not assert your mastery of evil by virtue of the power of goodness and thus become the master of all relations between the two of you? I predict that the good in you could overcome the evil in him if you gave it a fair and living chance."

He leaned closer, his voice carrying an intensity that caught Anaxand completely. "There is no adventure in the course of mortal existence more enthralling than to enjoy the exhilaration of becoming the material life partner with spiritual energy and divine truth in one of their triumphant struggles with error and evil. It is a marvelous and transforming experience to become the living channel of spiritual light to one who sits in spiritual darkness."

Jesus placed a hand on Anaxand's shoulder. "If you are more blessed with truth than is this man, his need should challenge you. Surely you are not the coward who could stand by on the seashore and watch a fellow man who could not swim perish! How much more of value is this man's soul floundering in darkness compared to his body drowning in water!"

Anaxand was mightily moved. That night he and his superior—the very foreman he had complained about—both sought Jesus's advice regarding the welfare of their souls.

Later, after the Christian message had been proclaimed in Caesarea, both men believed Philip's preaching and became prominent members of the church he founded. Anaxand would continue ministering light to those who sat in darkness until the days of Paul's imprisonment at Caesarea, when he perished by accident in the great slaughter of twenty thousand Jews while he was ministering to the suffering and dying.

But on this day in the shipyard, Anaxand was simply learning that evil is not overcome by resisting it, but by replacing it—becoming so filled with light that darkness has no place to hide.

During their evenings in Caesarea, Jesus and his friends strolled about on the beautiful wall that served as a promenade around the port. Ganid greatly enjoyed Jesus's explanations of the city's water system and the technique whereby the tides were utilized to flush the streets and sewers.

The young Indian was impressed with everything—the temple of Augustus with its colossal statue of the Roman emperor, the enormous amphitheater that could seat twenty thousand persons, the

Greek plays at the theater. These were the first exhibitions of their kind Ganid had ever witnessed, and he asked Jesus many questions about them.

But increasingly, Ganid was fascinated by something else: Jesus's interactions with ordinary people. Everywhere they went, Jesus seemed to find someone who needed help, guidance, or simply a compassionate ear. And Jesus gave himself to these encounters with complete attention, as though each person he met was the most important individual in the world.

One night Ganid finally asked the question directly: "Why do you occupy yourself so continuously with these visits with strangers?"

Jesus's answer was simple and profound. "Ganid, no man is a stranger to one who knows God. In the experience of finding the Father in heaven, you discover that all men are your brothers. And does it seem strange that one should enjoy the exhilaration of meeting a newly discovered brother? To become acquainted with one's brothers and sisters, to know their problems and to learn to love them, is the supreme experience of living."

The young man considered this. Then he asked another question: "What is the difference between the will of God and the human will—the act of choosing we all possess?"

They talked well into the night. In the course of the discussion, Jesus explained: "The will of God is the way of God—partnership with the choice of God in the face of any potential alternative. To do the will of God, therefore, is the progressive experience of becoming more and more like God, and God is the source and destiny of all that is good and beautiful and true."

He paused, making sure Ganid understood. "The will of man is the way of man—the sum and substance of that which a person chooses to be and do. Will is the deliberate choice of a self-conscious being which leads to decision and conduct based on intelligent reflection."

Ganid was beginning to grasp the pattern. Jesus was teaching him not just philosophy, but a way of living—a way of relating to God and to other human beings. Every encounter with strangers, every conversation by the seaside or in the shipyard, was part of this larger education.

At their inn in Caesarea, there also lodged a merchant from Mongolia. This Far-Easterner spoke Greek fairly well, and Jesus had several long visits with him. The Mongolian was deeply impressed with Jesus's philosophy of life and never forgot his words of wisdom regarding "the living of the heavenly life while on earth by means of daily submission to the will of the heavenly Father."

This merchant was a follower of Taoism, and he had thereby become a believer in the doctrine of a universal Deity. When he returned to Mongolia, he began teaching these advanced truths to his neighbors and business associates. As a direct result, his eldest son decided to become a Taoist priest. This young man exerted great influence on behalf of advanced truth throughout his lifetime and was followed by a son and a grandson who likewise were devotedly loyal to the doctrine of the One God—the Supreme Ruler of Heaven.

Jesus would never know the full reach of his influence during these travels. The Mongolian merchant returned home changed. Gadiah in Joppa became a pillar of the early church. Anaxand ministered to the dying during persecution. And these were only three among hundreds of people whose lives Jesus touched during his Mediterranean journey.

Each conversation, each encounter, each word of wisdom dropped into a receptive heart—all of it was planting seeds that would bear fruit across generations and continents.

As they finally set sail from Caesarea to Alexandria, Ganid was beginning to understand the full scope of what he was witnessing. His tutor was not merely an interpreter and translator. He was something far greater—a teacher whose wisdom transcended culture and religion, whose compassion embraced all humanity, whose understanding of God was both intimate and universal.

"You know more than the professors," Ganid would eventually tell Jesus in Alexandria. "You should stand up and tell them the great things you have told me."

But Jesus would only smile and reply, "The true teacher maintains his intellectual integrity by ever remaining a learner."

It was a lesson Ganid would remember all his life. His tutor—this Damascus scribe, this Jewish carpenter who spoke so many languages and knew so many crafts—was the greatest teacher he would ever encounter. Not because Jesus lectured or held forth with authority, but because he lived what he taught. He embodied the truth he proclaimed.

And that truth was simple: God loves all his children. Every human being is precious. No one is a stranger. The supreme experience of living is to know your brothers and sisters, to understand their problems, and to learn to love them.

It was a truth the world desperately needed. And Jesus was preparing, through these hundreds of personal encounters, to proclaim it to all humanity.

But not yet. For now, he was simply the Damascus scribe—a humble interpreter traveling with an Indian merchant, leaving transformed lives in his wake wherever he went.

The Mediterranean journey continued. Alexandria, Carthage, Rome, Athens—each city would bring new encounters, new teachings, new souls touched by the wisdom and compassion of this extraordinary man.

But the pattern was established in those first stops at Joppa and Caesarea. This was Jesus's method: one person at a time, one conversation at a time, one life at a time.

It was the method he would carry into his public ministry. And it was the method that would eventually change the world.[1]

12

ALEXANDRIA

The voyage from Caesarea to Alexandria was pleasant, the Mediterranean calm and welcoming. Ganid was delighted with the sea journey and kept Jesus busy answering an endless stream of questions about navigation, weather patterns, marine life, and the peoples they would encounter in Egypt.

As they approached Alexandria's harbor in the early morning, Ganid was thrilled by the sight of the great lighthouse of Pharos. The massive structure rose from an island that Alexander the Great had connected to the mainland by a causeway, creating two magnificent harbors and making Alexandria the maritime commercial crossroads of Africa, Asia, and Europe. The lighthouse was one of the seven wonders of the world—the forerunner of all subsequent lighthouses, a beacon of safety for ships across the treacherous waters.

Ganid stood at the rail, transfixed by the imposing tower with its fire burning at the top. Jesus stood beside him, watching the young man's face in the dawn light.

"You, my son," Jesus said quietly, "will be like this lighthouse when you return to India, even after your father is laid to rest. You will become like the light of life to those who sit about you in darkness, showing all who so desire the way to reach the harbor of salvation in safety."

Ganid squeezed Jesus's hand, his voice thick with emotion. "I will."

It was a prophetic moment. This young man from India, still in his teenage years, was being transformed by his travels with the Damascus scribe. He was learning not just languages and customs, but a way of seeing the world—a way of understanding God and humanity that would shape the rest of his life.

By mid-morning they were settled near the eastern end of Alexandria's great avenue—a street one hundred feet wide and five miles long that stretched from the harbor to the western limits of this magnificent city of one million people.

After a brief survey of Alexandria's chief attractions—the university, the royal mausoleum of Alexander, the palace, the temple of Neptune, the theater, and the gymnasium—Gonod addressed himself to his business affairs while Jesus and Ganid made their way to the great library.

Here was assembled the greatest collection of knowledge in the world: nearly one million manuscripts from every civilized land— Greece, Rome, Palestine, Parthia, India, China, and even distant Japan. Ganid saw the largest collection of Indian literature that existed anywhere, and his eyes widened with wonder at the sheer scope of human learning gathered in this single place.

They spent time in the library each day throughout their stay in Alexandria. Jesus told Ganid about the translation of the Hebrew scriptures into Greek that had been accomplished at this very location centuries earlier—the Septuagint, which had made the Jewish sacred writings accessible to the Greek-speaking world.

But their discussions ranged far beyond Jewish scripture. They talked about all the religions of the world, examining the sacred texts and philosophical traditions of every major culture. Jesus endeavored to point out to Ganid the truth contained in each religious system, always careful to highlight what united rather than what divided humanity's various attempts to know God.

"The Jews," Jesus explained, "eventually came to portray a clearer recognition of the Lord God of Israel as the Universal Father in heaven than any other world religion. Their understanding grew through revelation and covenant, and they preserved this knowledge even when other nations lost sight of it."

Under Jesus's direction, Ganid began making a remarkable collection. He copied out passages from the sacred writings of all those religions which recognized a Universal Deity—even when they also acknowledged lesser gods or spirits. It was painstaking work, requiring careful translation and thoughtful selection.

After much discussion, Jesus and Ganid concluded that the Romans had no real God in their religion—their worship was hardly more than emperor veneration. The Greeks, they decided, had developed sophisticated philosophy but lacked a religion centered on a personal God. The mystery cults they discarded as too confused and contradictory, their concepts of deity apparently borrowed and distorted from older traditions.

Ganid would not finalize this collection until near the end of their sojourn in Rome, months later. But when he did, he was astonished to discover something profound: the best authors of the world's sacred literature all more or less clearly recognized the existence of an eternal God. Despite vast differences in culture, language, and ritual, there was remarkable agreement regarding God's character and his relationship with humanity.

The library revealed what the world's theologians had often obscured: beneath the surface differences, humanity's spiritual instincts pointed toward the same ultimate reality—a loving, eternal Father who cared for all his children.

Jesus and Ganid also spent considerable time at Alexandria's museum. This was not merely a collection of rare objects but rather a university devoted to fine art, science, and literature. Learned professors gave daily lectures here, and in those days Alexandria was recognized as the intellectual center of the Western world.

Day by day, Jesus interpreted the lectures for Ganid, translating Greek and Latin into the young man's native tongue and adding context that helped him understand the cultural assumptions behind various arguments.

One day during their second week, after a particularly dense lecture on metaphysics, Ganid could contain himself no longer. He exclaimed to Jesus, "Teacher Joshua, you know more than these professors! You should stand up and tell them the great things you have told me. They are befogged by much thinking. I shall speak to my father and have him arrange it."

Jesus smiled at the young man's enthusiasm. "You are an admiring pupil," he said gently, "but these teachers are not minded that you and I should instruct them. The pride of unspiritualized learning is a treacherous thing in human experience."

It was a lesson Ganid needed to hear. Intellectual achievement without spiritual insight could lead to arrogance rather than wisdom. The truly wise person never stopped learning, never claimed to have exhausted truth, never looked down on others for their ignorance.

Alexandria itself embodied both the glory and the danger of pure intellectualism. Here was the blended culture of East and West, Greek thought married to Egyptian tradition, with Jewish, Roman, Persian, and Indian influences all mixing in a cosmopolitan stew. It was the largest and most magnificent city in the world after Rome—a showcase of human learning and achievement.

Yet for all its splendor, Alexandria had not found God. Its philosophers debated endlessly about the nature of reality while missing the simple truth that Jesus carried: God is a loving Father who desires relationship with his children. All the learning in the library, all the lectures in the museum, all the philosophical sophistication in the world could not substitute for this direct, personal knowledge of the divine.

Among the many businessmen with whom Gonod transacted affairs was a certain Jewish banker named Alexander. His brother, Philo, was a famous religious philosopher of that time—engaged in the laudable but exceedingly difficult task of harmonizing Greek philosophy with Hebrew theology.

Ganid and Jesus talked much about Philo's teachings. They had hoped to attend some of his lectures, but throughout their stay in Alexandria, this famous Hellenistic Jew lay sick in bed. It was a disappointment, though Jesus later told Ganid that Philo's approach—trying to force Greek and Hebrew thought into artificial harmony—missed something essential. Philosophy and religion served different purposes. One addressed the mind, the other the soul. The attempt to make them perfectly congruent often distorted both.

Jesus commended much in Greek philosophy to Ganid, particularly the Stoic doctrines with their emphasis on virtue, duty, and living in harmony with nature. But he impressed upon the young man a crucial truth: these systems of belief were religions only in the sense that they led people to find God and enjoy a living experience of knowing the Eternal. Philosophy could point the way, but it could not substitute for the journey itself.

The night before they were to depart Alexandria, Ganid and Jesus had a long visit with one of the government professors at the university— a man who lectured on Plato's teachings. Jesus served as interpreter, translating the conversation but injecting no teachings of his own in refutation of the Greek philosophy. Gonod was away on business that evening.

After the professor departed, teacher and pupil had a long and intimate conversation about Plato's doctrines. Jesus gave qualified approval to some of the Greek teachings—particularly the theory that material things are imperfect reflections of invisible but more substantial spiritual realities. There was truth in this idea. The physical world did indeed point beyond itself to deeper meanings.

But Jesus sought to lay a more trustworthy foundation for Ganid's thinking. So he began a careful explanation concerning the nature of reality in the universe.

"The source of all reality," Jesus explained, "is the Infinite God. The material things of our finite creation are reflections in time and space of God's eternal patterns and his divine mind. Causation in the physical world, self-consciousness in the intellectual world, and progressing selfhood in the spiritual world—these realities, when combined and experienced, point toward ultimate truth."

He paused, making sure Ganid was following. "But in an ever-changing universe, God himself is changeless. All things may change —even things of great value and quality—but God remains constant. He is the one fixed point in a cosmos of motion."

Ganid leaned forward, fascinated. "What is the highest level we can reach?"

"The highest level a finite creature can achieve," Jesus replied, "is the recognition of the Universal Father—truly knowing God as he is. And even then, such beings continue experiencing change in the physical world and growth in spiritual awareness. Only in perfect harmony of will can the creature become one with the Creator. And such unity is attained by consistently conforming one's personal will to the divine will. The desire to do the Father's will must be supreme in the soul and dominant over the mind."

Jesus used an analogy to make his point clearer. "A one-eyed person can never visualize depth of perspective. Neither can purely material scientists nor purely spiritual mystics correctly comprehend the full truth of universe reality. All true values are concealed in depth of recognition—you need multiple perspectives to see the whole."

He continued, his voice taking on greater intensity. "Mindless causes cannot create refined complexity from crude simplicity. Neither can experience devoid of spirit produce the divine characters that survive death. The one attribute of the universe which most clearly reveals God is his unending creative giving of personality—the gift of identity that can survive unlimited change and retain itself through all transformations."

Ganid struggled to grasp this profound concept. "You're saying that our personalities—our identities—can persist even as everything else changes?"

"Exactly," Jesus confirmed. "Personality is that cosmic endowment which can coexist with unlimited change while retaining its identity in the very presence of all such changes."

He elaborated on the nature of life itself. "Life is an adaptation of God's creative purpose to the demands and possibilities of each situation. It comes into being through divine will and spiritual activation. The meaning of life is its adaptability. The value of life is its capacity for progress—even to the heights of God-consciousness."

Jesus's voice grew more serious. "Misadaptation of life to the universe results in discord. Final divergence of personality will from the flow of universal purpose leads to isolation and segregation. But when the soul genuinely seeks God with whole-hearted devotion, when truth becomes more than theory and actually guides behavior—then real spiritual progress occurs."

They talked long into the night, Jesus patiently answering Ganid's questions, clarifying difficult concepts, using analogies from everyday experience to illuminate abstract truths.

By the time they finally retired, Ganid had received one of the most comprehensive discourses on reality that Jesus would deliver during his entire Mediterranean journey. It was not the simplified teaching appropriate for crowds, but the deep philosophy suited to a sincere student ready to grapple with ultimate questions.

The next morning, they departed Alexandria by boat. Ganid stood at the rail as the great lighthouse receded into the distance, its beacon still visible even in daylight. He thought about Jesus's words from their first morning in Alexandria—about becoming like a lighthouse, a source of illumination for those in darkness.

He thought about the library and its million manuscripts, representing humanity's collective attempt to understand the world and find meaning. He thought about the professors at the museum, brilliant and learned but often missing the simple truths that Jesus carried so effortlessly.

Most of all, he thought about the conversation they'd had the previous night—about the nature of reality, the persistence of personality, the importance of aligning one's will with God's will. It was heady stuff for a seventeen-year-old, but Ganid felt ready for it. His tutor treated him as an intellectual equal, worthy of the deepest truths.

As Alexandria faded from view, Ganid realized that he was being given an education unlike any other person on earth had ever received. He was learning directly from someone who didn't just know about God through study or speculation, but who seemed to know God personally, intimately, with absolute certainty.

He didn't yet understand the full truth—that his tutor was not merely a wise man but something far greater. For now, Ganid was simply grateful to be traveling with the Damascus scribe, learning from him day by day, being transformed by his wisdom and his compassion.

Their journey continued westward, toward Crete and then Carthage and eventually Rome. More cities, more encounters, more teachings lay ahead.

But Alexandria would remain special in Ganid's memory—the city of learning where he had received some of the deepest instruction of his life, the place where a wise teacher had explained to an eager student the very nature of reality itself.

The lighthouse of Pharos would eventually crumble and fall. The great library would burn. The museum and its learned professors would fade into history.

But the truths Jesus taught would endure. And Ganid, when he returned to India after his father's death, would indeed become like a lighthouse—shining the light of divine truth into the darkness, helping others find their way to the harbor of salvation.[1]

13

THE ISLAND OF CRETE

They came to Crete with no agenda save to play. After months of steady travel, teaching, and ministry to individuals across the eastern Mediterranean, the three companions needed rest. They would walk the island, climb its mountains, and simply breathe the mountain air. The Cretans of that time carried a dark reputation among surrounding peoples—they were known as liars, deceivers, and worse. Yet Jesus saw past the cultural prejudice to the souls beneath, and during their sojourn on the island, he and Ganid won many to higher levels of thinking and living. They were laying foundation stones for a harvest they would never see—when the first preachers from Jerusalem arrived years later, they would find soil already prepared.

It was on a mountainside in Crete that Gonod finally asked the questions that had been building in his mind for months. He had watched this Damascus scribe with growing wonder—the wisdom that flowed so naturally, the way he seemed to understand not just languages but the very hearts of those he spoke with, the peculiar authority in his voice when he spoke of God.

Gonod was a sophisticated man, wealthy and well-traveled. He knew the religious teachers of his own land, had heard the rabbis in

Jerusalem, had conversed with Greek philosophers in their academies. But he had never encountered anyone like Joshua ben Joseph.

"Teacher," Gonod began carefully, "I must confess something. My son believes everything you tell him, and I—" He paused, searching for words. "I never knew they had such a religion even in Jerusalem, much less in Damascus."

It was the opening of a conversation that would continue for the rest of their journey. Gonod was beginning to understand that whatever this young man possessed, it went far deeper than scholarly learning. There was something living in his words, something that made ancient truths feel immediate and real.

Before they left the island, Gonod made his proposal: "Come back to India with us. My son has learned more from you in these months than he could learn in years of formal schooling. I can offer you a position in my household, or help you establish yourself in Bombay. You need not answer now—but consider it."

Ganid's face lit up at his father's words. The possibility that his teacher might remain with them permanently was more than he had dared hope for.

Jesus smiled at them both with genuine warmth. "Your offer honors me," he said. "Let me think on it as we continue our journey."

But in his heart, he already knew the answer. His path led elsewhere, to a work these kind souls could not yet imagine.

One afternoon, as they walked through an olive grove, Ganid voiced a question that had troubled him: "Teacher Joshua, you have such wisdom and power with words. You could draw crowds, establish a school, become famous throughout the empire. Why do you not devote yourself to the work of a public teacher?"

Jesus stopped walking and turned to face the young man. "My son," he said, "everything must await the coming of its time. You are born into the world, but no amount of anxiety and no manifestation of impatience will help you to grow up. You must, in all such matters, wait upon time. Time alone will ripen the green fruit upon the tree. Season follows season and sundown follows sunrise only with the passing of time. I am now on the way to Rome with you and your father, and that is sufficient for today. My tomorrow is wholly in the hands of my Father in heaven."

Then he told them the story of Moses—how the prince of Egypt had to wait forty years in the wilderness, tending sheep and learning patience, before he was ready for the work God had prepared for him. "Those years seemed wasted to Moses at the time," Jesus explained, "yet they were essential. The man who led Israel out of bondage could not have been the impulsive prince who killed an Egyptian guard in anger. That man had to die in the desert so that a different man could emerge—one who had learned to wait upon God's timing."

Ganid absorbed this teaching quietly, but he didn't fully understand. He was seventeen, and the young rarely grasp the value of waiting. Still, the story planted a seed that would grow throughout his life.

The following incident at Fair Havens seared itself into Ganid's memory so powerfully that decades later, as an old man in India, he would still speak of it—and still wonder at what he had witnessed that day.

They were walking through the town when they heard screaming ahead. A slave girl—she couldn't have been more than fourteen—was being assaulted on the public highway by a drunken man. The degenerate had her by the arm and was striking her repeatedly while shouting incoherently.

Jesus moved before Ganid even registered what was happening. One moment his teacher was beside him, the next he was between the attacker and the girl, pulling her free and putting himself in harm's way.

The frightened child clung to Jesus while the madman, enraged at being thwarted, launched himself forward with clenched fists. But Jesus extended his right arm—that powerful arm that had swung hammers in his father's shop for years—and held the man at a safe distance. It wasn't a strike or even a shove. It was simply an immovable barrier that the drunk could not pass.

The man raged and swung wildly at the air, cursing and trying to reach Jesus or the girl. But Jesus stood firm, his arm extended, his face calm, waiting. He didn't speak. He didn't threaten. He just held the man at bay with that quiet, implacable strength until finally, inevitably, the drunk exhausted himself. His blows became weaker, then stopped altogether. He stumbled backward, breathing heavily, then turned and staggered away.

Only then did Jesus lower his arm.

Though none of them could speak the girl's language, they understood her tears of gratitude and escorted her home.

That evening, Ganid couldn't contain his confusion. "Teacher, why did you not strike that man? He deserved to be beaten! He should have been struck at least as many times as he struck that poor girl!"

Jesus tried to explain—about meeting violence with violence only creating more violence, about how striking the man would have satisfied Ganid's sense of justice but would not have helped the girl or changed the attacker's heart. But Jesus could see his young friend wasn't fully satisfied with the answer.

What Ganid couldn't know was that the scene he'd witnessed was extraordinary in Jesus's life for another reason—it was probably as near a personal physical encounter with his fellows as Jesus would have throughout his entire life in the flesh. The carpenter from Nazareth, who could have struck with devastating force, had chosen instead to simply wait, to hold the space for rage to exhaust itself.

Years later, when Ganid had children of his own, he would remember that afternoon and finally understand. And the memory of that slave girl's rescue would fuel his lifelong efforts to change the caste system in his native India. One girl, one rescue, one afternoon—and the ripples would spread across an ocean and down through generations.

They went up into the mountains, seeking the coolness of higher elevations and the quiet of less-traveled paths. It was there, on a trail winding through rocky highlands, that Jesus encountered the young man who would become one of Crete's most significant Christian leaders.

They saw him from a distance—a solitary figure sitting on a boulder, head down, the very picture of dejection. As they drew closer, Jesus signaled Gonod and Ganid to wait, and he approached alone.

"Greetings, my friend!" Jesus called out cheerfully. "Why so downcast on such a beautiful day? If something has happened to distress you, perhaps I can in some manner assist you. At any rate it affords me real pleasure to proffer my services."

The young man barely looked up. He mumbled something inaudible and turned away, clearly wishing to be left alone.

Jesus tried again, taking a different approach. "I understand you come up in these hills to get away from folks; so, of course, you do not want to talk with me, but I would like to know whether you are familiar with these mountains; do you know the direction of the trails? And, perchance, could you inform me as to the best route to Phenix?"

This question penetrated where the offer of help had not. The young man looked up, and Jesus saw a face marked by long-term sadness—the kind that comes not from a single blow but from years of accumulated defeat. But the technical question about trails sparked something. This, at least, he knew. This he could answer.

And so he did. In detail. He marked out all the trails on the ground with a stick, explained every fork and landmark, described the terrain and estimated the walking times. For perhaps ten minutes, as he instructed this stranger on the best route to Phenix, he forgot his misery. He was competent at something, useful, able to help.

When he finished, Jesus thanked him warmly and began to turn away as if to leave. But after a few steps, he stopped and turned back.

"I well know you wish to be left alone with your disconsolation," Jesus said, his voice gentle but firm, "but it would be neither kind nor fair for me to receive such generous help from you as to how best to find my way to Phenix and then unthinkingly to go away from you without making the least effort to answer your appealing request for help and guidance regarding the best route to the goal of destiny which you seek in your heart while you tarry here on the mountainside."

The young man looked up, startled. "But—but I did not ask you for anything—"

Jesus moved closer and laid a gentle hand on his shoulder. "No, son, not with words but with longing looks did you appeal to my heart. My boy, to one who loves his fellows there is an eloquent appeal for help in your countenance of discouragement and despair."

The dam broke. The young man's face crumpled, and in that moment all his carefully maintained walls came down. Here was someone who saw him—really saw him—and cared.

"Sit down with me," Jesus said, settling himself on the ground, "while I tell you of the trails of service and happiness highways which lead from the sorrows of self to the joys of loving activities in the brotherhood of men and in the service of the God of heaven."

By this time the young man very much desired to talk. He knelt at Jesus's feet, the words pouring out—his father's death when he was twelve, the feelings of helplessness and inferiority that had haunted him since childhood, the way difficult circumstances seemed to pile up, the sense that he was simply not equipped for life, that he had been given a burden too heavy to carry.

Jesus listened until the outpouring subsided. Then he spoke with unusual force.

"My friend, arise! Stand up like a man!"

The command was so unexpected, delivered with such authority, that the young man scrambled to his feet almost involuntarily.

"You may be surrounded with small enemies and be retarded by many obstacles," Jesus continued, "but the big things and the real things of this world and the universe are on your side. The sun rises every morning to salute you just as it does the most powerful and prosperous man on earth. Look—you have a strong body and powerful muscles—your physical equipment is better than the average. Of course, it is just about useless while you sit out here on the mountainside and grieve over your misfortunes, real and fancied. But you could do great things with your body if you would hasten off to where great things are waiting to be done."

Jesus took a step closer. "You are trying to run away from your unhappy self, but it cannot be done. You and your problems of living are real; you cannot escape them as long as you live. But look again, your mind is clear and capable. Your strong body has an intelligent mind to direct it. Set your mind at work to solve its problems; teach your intellect to work for you; refuse longer to be dominated by fear like an unthinking animal."

The young man was standing straighter now, something kindling in his eyes.

"Your mind should be your courageous ally in the solution of your life problems rather than a the bond-servant of depression and defeat. But most valuable of all, your potential of real achievement is the spirit which lives within you, and which will stimulate and inspire your mind to control itself and activate the body if you will release it from the fetters of fear and thus enable your spiritual nature to begin your deliverance from the evils of inaction by the power-presence of living faith."

Jesus's voice rose with conviction: "And then, forthwith, will this faith vanquish fear of men by the compelling presence of that new and all-dominating love of your fellows which will so soon fill your soul to overflowing because of the consciousness which has been born in your heart that you are a child of God."

The young man was weeping now, but these were different tears—tears of release rather than despair.

"This day, my son, you are to be reborn, re-established as a man of faith, courage, and devoted service to man, for God's sake. And when you become so readjusted to life within yourself, you become likewise readjusted to the universe; you have been born again—born of the spirit—and henceforth will your whole life become one of victorious accomplishment. Trouble will invigorate you; disappointment will spur you on; difficulties will challenge you; and obstacles will stimu-late you."

Jesus gripped the young man's shoulders. "Arise, young man! Say farewell to the life of cringing fear and fleeing cowardice. Hasten back to duty and live your life as a son of God, a mortal dedicated to the ennobling service of man on earth and destined to the superb and eternal service of God in eternity.

The transformation was immediate and visible. The young man stood taller, his shoulders back, his face lifted. The depression that had settled on him like a physical weight seemed to fall away. He wasn't suddenly free of all his problems—but he was free of the belief that his problems were unconquerable.

His name was Fortune, and the encounter on that mountainside set the course for the rest of his life. When Paul later sent Titus to Crete to reorganize the churches there, he found the Cretan believers in remarkable condition—largely due to the leadership of this man who had been reborn in a single afternoon on a mountain trail.

When they finally left Crete, rested and refreshed, they made ready one afternoon to sail for Carthage in northern Africa. The plan was to stop for two days at Cyrene on the way.

It was in Cyrene that they heard shouting in the street—a young boy had been injured when a loaded oxcart broke down, and he was trapped beneath it. Jesus and Ganid rushed to help. Together they lifted the broken cart enough for others to pull the boy free, and then they carried him home to his anxious mother.

The boy's father came running soon after—a big man, a common laborer with powerful shoulders. His name was Simon, and his gratitude was effusive. He insisted they stay for a meal, tried to pay them, wanted to know how he could repay such kindness to his son Rufus.

"Your thanks are payment enough," Jesus told him. "Your son will recover well. See that he rests for a few days."

Simon walked them back to the docks, still thanking them, still overwhelmed that strangers would go out of their way for a carpenter's son.

He could not possibly have known that in less than four years he would be pressed into service by a Roman soldier in Jerusalem. He would be forced to carry a cross for a condemned man stumbling through the streets toward Golgotha. And though he did not recognize it, the face he would see when he picked up that cross would be the face of the stranger who had once carried his son home in Cyrene.[1]

14

ACROSS THE EMPIRE

The voyage from Crete to Carthage revealed a different side of Jesus to his traveling companions. For the first time since they had met him, he talked freely about things other than religion—social customs, political arrangements, commerce and trade. Gonod and Ganid discovered that this Damascus scribe was a gifted storyteller, and they kept him busy with tales of his early life in Galilee. They learned that he had been raised not in Jerusalem or Damascus, as they had assumed, but in a small village in the northern hill country. The stories of his childhood—his large family, his father's carpentry shop, the views from the Nazareth ridge—made him seem more human, more approachable, than he had sometimes appeared when speaking of divine things.

During one of these casual conversations, Ganid asked a question that had been forming in his mind throughout their journey: "Teacher, I have noticed that most people we meet are drawn to you. They want to talk with you, to be near you. How does one make friends so easily?"

Jesus smiled at the directness of the question. "Become interested in your fellows," he said simply. "Learn how to love them and watch for the opportunity to do something for them which you are sure they want done." Then he quoted an old Jewish proverb that Ganid would remember for the rest of his life: "A man who would have friends must show himself friendly."

It was such practical wisdom—not abstract philosophy, but something a young man could actually do. Ganid began watching Jesus more carefully after that, studying how he approached people, how he listened, how he seemed to sense what each person needed most.

———

At Carthage, the ancient city that had once rivaled Rome itself, Jesus encountered a Mithraic priest who was genuinely seeking truth. The man had been educated at Alexandria and possessed a sophisticated mind that craved understanding of the deeper mysteries. When he learned that the Damascus scribe could discuss philosophical matters with unusual depth, he sought him out for conversation.

Their talk turned to the nature of time and eternity—questions that had occupied the Persian's mind for years. Jesus spoke to him in language suited to his philosophical training, yet with a clarity that cut through the obscurities that usually surrounded such topics.

Time, Jesus explained, is the stream of events as perceived by conscious beings. It is a name given to the succession of events whereby they can be recognized and separated from one another. The universe of space appears as a time-related phenomenon when viewed from any position within it. Motion and time are connected— the movement of time is revealed only in relation to something that does not move in space.

The priest listened intently, recognizing that he was hearing concepts far beyond the usual discussions of such matters.

But God, Jesus continued, transcends both time and space. And remarkably, human personality—when indwelt and oriented by the divine spirit—is the only physical reality that can transcend the material sequence of events. The spirit within gives mortals a connection to the eternal.

Animals do not sense time as humans do. But as human beings grow spiritually, their perception of time changes. What once appeared as a mere succession of events begins to be seen as a whole, a perfectly related cycle. The consciousness that perceives only the linear sequence of events gradually awakens to what might be called circular simultaneity—seeing the whole pattern rather than just the passing moments.

The priest's eyes widened. This was unlike anything he had heard from the teachers of Mithras or the philosophers of Alexandria.

Space too, Jesus said, is not what most people assume. It is not empty, not merely an intellectual concept describing how objects relate to one another. Mind alone can partially transcend space, functioning independently of material objects. And as consciousness expands through spiritual growth, the concepts of time and space themselves are transformed, enlarged beyond anything the material mind can initially grasp.

All of this, Jesus assured him, would become experientially real to those who pursue the ascending path toward God. The time-space concepts of a mind rooted in material existence are destined to undergo successive enlargements as personality ascends through the levels of universal reality. What seems abstract philosophy now would one day be living experience.

The Mithraic priest returned to his duties a changed man. He had come seeking intellectual answers and had received instead a glimpse of realities that made his previous questions seem small. He would spend years pondering what he had heard that afternoon in Carthage.

The first stop on the way to Italy was the island of Malta. Here Jesus encountered a young man named Claudus whose despair had brought him to the edge of self-destruction.

They met by chance—or what seemed like chance—and began talking. Claudus poured out his troubles to this sympathetic stranger. Life had defeated him. He had failed at everything he attempted. His family had given up on him. He saw no reason to continue.

Jesus listened with full attention, asking questions that showed he genuinely understood the weight of the young man's burden. Then, as he had done with Fortune on the Cretan mountainside, he began to speak truth into the darkness.

The conversation lasted hours. When it ended, Claudus stood straighter. Something had shifted inside him. "I will face life like a man," he declared. "I am through playing the coward. I will go back to my people and begin all over again."

And he did. Shortly after, Claudus became an enthusiastic preacher among the Cynics, whose philosophy had preserved more of the ancient truth about God than most schools of thought. Still later, he joined hands with Peter himself, proclaiming the new faith in Rome and Naples. After Peter's death, he carried the gospel all the way to Spain.

But to his dying day, Claudus never knew that the Damascus scribe who had talked him back from the brink of suicide was the same Jesus whom he proclaimed as the world's Deliverer. He never connected the kind stranger on Malta with the risen Christ he preached. The seeds and the harvest belonged to different seasons of his life, and he never saw them as one.

At Syracuse, on the island of Sicily, they spent a full week. The city was ancient and beautiful, but Jesus's attention was drawn not to its monuments but to a man named Ezra.

Ezra was a Jew who had drifted far from the faith of his fathers. He kept a tavern where the travelers stopped, and from the moment they arrived, he was captivated by Jesus's manner—the authority combined with gentleness, the evident learning worn so lightly.

One evening, Ezra worked up the courage to approach him. "Teacher," he said, "I can see that you know the ways of God. I want to be a true son of Abraham, but I cannot find God." His voice carried years of failed attempts and mounting despair.

Jesus regarded him with compassion. "If you truly want to find God," he said, "that desire is in itself evidence that you have already found him."

Ezra blinked, not understanding.

"Your trouble is not that you cannot find God," Jesus continued, "for the Father has already found you. Your trouble is simply that you do not know God."

Then he quoted from the prophets that Ezra had learned as a child but had long since forgotten: "Have you not read in Jeremiah, 'You shall seek me and find me when you shall search for me with all your heart'? And again, does not this same prophet say, 'And I will give you a heart to know me, that I am the Lord, and you shall belong to my people, and I will be your God'?"

The words struck Ezra like physical blows—not painful, but powerful, breaking through walls he had built over years of spiritual failure.

"And have you not also read in the Scriptures," Jesus added, "where it says, 'He looks down upon men, and if any will say: I have sinned and perverted that which was right, and it profited me not, then will God deliver that man's soul from darkness, and he shall see the light'?"

That night, Ezra found God. Or rather, he finally recognized that God had been seeking him all along, waiting for him to stop running and turn around. The tavern keeper's life was transformed. Later, in partnership with a wealthy Greek convert, he built the first Christian church in Syracuse.

At Messina, they stopped for only one day—just long enough to change a life.

A small boy was selling fruit near the docks. Jesus bought some from him and fell into conversation. The child was perhaps ten years old, bright-eyed and curious, supporting his family through his small commerce. Jesus saw in him a soul ready to receive truth, even if the boy was too young to understand it fully.

As they parted, Jesus placed his hand on the boy's shoulder and looked into his eyes. "Farewell, my lad. Be of good courage as you grow up to manhood, and after you have fed the body, learn how also to feed the soul. And my Father in heaven will be with you and go before you."

The boy never forgot those words or the kindly look that accompanied them. Years later, he became a devotee of Mithras, seeking the divine through the only path he knew. But the seed planted that day in Messina eventually bore fruit—he found his way to the Christian faith, recognizing in its teachings the same spirit he had sensed in a stranger's blessing long ago.

At last they reached Naples and felt they were not far from their destination. Gonod had much business to transact in the city, and while he was occupied, Jesus and Ganid explored together.

By now, Ganid had become adept at spotting those who appeared to be in need. It was a skill Jesus had taught him without formal instruction—simply by example, by the way he moved through crowds with eyes that saw not just faces but souls. They found much poverty in Naples and distributed many alms.

But one encounter puzzled Ganid deeply. After giving a coin to a street beggar, Jesus refused to pause and speak with him as he usually did. When Ganid asked why, Jesus said something that troubled him:

"Why waste words upon one who cannot perceive the meaning of what you say? The spirit of the Father cannot teach and save one who has no capacity for sonship."

Ganid struggled with this. It seemed harsh, unlike his teacher's usual compassion. What he couldn't fully grasp was that Jesus saw something in this particular man that Ganid could not—a mind so damaged that the capacity for spiritual response no longer existed. There was no cruelty in Jesus's words, only the recognition of a tragic reality. The coin could ease physical hunger; words of spiritual truth required a mind capable of receiving them.

It was a hard lesson, and Ganid never entirely understood it. But he remembered it, turning it over in his mind for years afterward—the recognition that even infinite love must work within the limitations of those it seeks to reach.

<hr>

From Naples they traveled to Capua, stopping for three days, and then set out on the final leg of their journey. The Appian Way stretched before them—that magnificent Roman road that connected the southern regions to the capital itself. They walked beside their pack animals, three travelers among many on that ancient highway, all moving toward the same destination.

Rome. The mistress of empire. The greatest city in all the world.

All three were anxious to see it—Gonod for business, Ganid for wonder, and Jesus for reasons he shared with no one. Somewhere in that vast city, souls were waiting to be touched. Conversations were waiting to be had. Seeds were waiting to be planted.

The Damascus scribe walked the Roman road with steady steps, his face turned toward the city that ruled the world. But his thoughts reached further than Rome—to a work that would one day transform the empire from within, beginning with individual hearts changed one at a time.

The road to Rome was nearly ended. The road to Golgotha had not yet begun.

Between them lay months of ministry in the eternal city, encounters that would echo through centuries, and a young Indian's education in what it truly meant to love one's fellow man.[1]

15

THE IMPERIAL CITY

GONOD CARRIED LETTERS OF INTRODUCTION FROM INDIAN ROYALTY, and within three days of their arrival, he secured an audience with Tiberius Caesar himself. Jesus accompanied Gonod and Ganid to the imperial palace.

The emperor was notoriously suspicious and prone to dark moods, but that day he seemed genuinely interested in his visitors. He asked about their travels, their impressions of the empire, their observations of the peoples they had encountered. The conversation lasted longer than such audiences typically did.

As the three departed, Tiberius turned to an aide and remarked, "If I had that fellow's kingly bearing and gracious manner, I would be a real emperor, eh?"

The comment would have astonished anyone who knew the true identity of the quiet interpreter. The ruler of the known world had glimpsed something in Jesus that surpassed even imperial authority. But the moment passed unremarked, and the Jewish scribe was forgotten by the court.

Gonod had extensive business in Rome, and he wanted Ganid to begin learning the family's commercial interests. So while father and son attended to trade matters—often with one of Gonod's employees serving as interpreter—Jesus found himself with considerable free time.

He used it deliberately. He walked the great forum where Roman political and commercial life converged. He climbed to the Capitolium and stood before the temple of Jupiter, Juno, and Minerva, contemplating how even the masters of the world groped in spiritual darkness. He explored the Palatine Hill with its imperial residence and its Greek and Latin libraries.

Rome drew people from everywhere. The empire's reach extended across southern Europe, through Asia Minor and Syria, down into Egypt and across northwest Africa. Representatives of virtually every race and culture on earth could be found in its capital. This was precisely why Jesus had agreed to make the journey—to encounter humanity in all its diversity.

He learned much during those months. But his most significant work involved the religious leaders of the city.

Within his first week, Jesus had identified and befriended the most thoughtful teachers among the Cynics, the Stoics, and the mystery religions—particularly the Mithraic cult. He seemed to know that messengers would eventually come to Rome proclaiming the kingdom of heaven, and he set about preparing the ground for their arrival.

He selected thirty-two of these teachers for special attention: five Stoics, eleven Cynics, and sixteen leaders of mystery cults. Over the following months, he spent his free hours in deep conversation with them.

His approach was unlike anything they had experienced. He never criticized their beliefs or pointed out their errors. Instead, he found the truth already present in their teachings and helped them see it more clearly. He expanded and illuminated what was already good until, gradually, the enhanced truth displaced the errors that had surrounded it. These men and women were being prepared—without knowing it—to recognize similar truths when Christian missionaries eventually arrived.

The results were remarkable. Of the thirty-two religious leaders Jesus befriended in Rome, thirty became instrumental in establishing Christianity in the city. Some helped convert the chief Mithraic temple into Rome's first Christian church.

Years later, Peter and Paul would hear stories about a mysterious Damascus scribe who had somehow prepared the way for their message. Paul wondered if this scribe might be the same man he had known as "the tentmaker of Antioch." Peter, hearing descriptions of the Damascus teacher, briefly wondered if it could have been Jesus—but dismissed the thought, certain that the Master had never visited Rome.

Early in his stay, Jesus spent an entire night in conversation with Angamon, the leading Stoic teacher. Angamon would later become one of Paul's closest allies and a pillar of the Roman church.

They discussed the relationship between science and spirituality. Jesus taught him that true values must be sought in spiritual reality, not material observation alone. The scientist, working within his proper domain, discovers relationships between physical facts—but the moment he declares himself a materialist or an idealist, he has stepped beyond science into philosophy.

Jesus warned that material progress without corresponding moral and spiritual growth could eventually threaten civilization itself. A purely materialistic culture, he said, carries within it the seeds of its own destruction.

But scientists and spiritual seekers need not be enemies. Both stand accountable to human need. Both must justify their existence through service to human progress.

Mardus led the Cynics of Rome, and he too became a close friend of the Damascus scribe. Their conversations ranged widely, but the most important addressed Mardus's persistent question about the nature of good and evil.

Good and evil, Jesus explained, are words describing how humans understand reality at different levels. The lazy person accepts current social customs as the standard of good. The spiritually stagnant person accepts inherited religious traditions. But the soul that seeks to survive beyond this life must make living choices between good and evil as defined by genuine spiritual standards—standards established by the divine spirit that dwells in every human heart.

Goodness and truth are always relative, always contrasted with their opposites. It is the perception of these qualities that enables growing souls to make the choices essential for eternal survival.

The person who blindly follows scientific consensus, social convention, or religious authority risks losing both moral freedom and spiritual liberty. Such a soul becomes merely an intellectual parrot, a social automaton, a slave to external authority.

True goodness always grows toward greater freedom—moral self-realization and spiritual development through discovery of the divine spirit within. An experience is good when it deepens appreciation of beauty, strengthens moral will, sharpens discernment of truth, expands capacity for love and service, elevates spiritual ideals, and unifies human purposes with eternal divine plans.

Evil exists as a possibility because moral choice requires alternatives. But potential evil serves the purposes of moral growth without requiring that evil become actual. Evil becomes real only when a moral mind deliberately chooses it.

Nabon was a Greek Jew who led Rome's chief Mithraic temple. He held many conversations with Jesus, but the discussion that changed him most concerned the nature of truth and faith.

Nabon had hoped to convert Jesus to Mithraism—perhaps even send him back to Palestine as a Mithraic teacher. He did not realize that Jesus was preparing him to receive a very different message.

Truth, Jesus taught him, cannot be captured in definitions. It can only be lived. Truth always exceeds knowledge. Knowledge deals with observed facts, but truth transcends the material to embrace wisdom, human experience, and spiritual reality.

People tend to crystallize science, formulate philosophy, and dogmatize truth because they fear change and dread the unknown. They resist adjusting their habits of thought.

But revealed truth—truth personally discovered—brings supreme joy to the human soul. It emerges from the partnership between the human mind and the indwelling divine spirit. The soul that hungers for goodness, that develops a single-minded purpose to do the Father's will, to find God and become like him—such a soul is assured eternal survival.

Yet truth cannot be possessed without faith. Human thoughts, wisdom, ethics, and ideals never rise higher than faith allows. And genuine faith rests on deep reflection, honest self-examination, and unflinching moral awareness.

Faith releases the divine spark within—the immortal seed that makes eternal survival possible. Human life continues because it has a cosmic purpose: finding God. The faith-activated soul cannot stop short of this goal. And having achieved it, having become like God, it can never end.

Nabon was profoundly moved. These ideas burned within him for years, and when Christian preachers eventually arrived in Rome, he became one of their most valuable allies.

***

Jesus did not spend all his time with religious teachers. He sought out people from every level of Roman society, wanting to understand how they lived and thought. And in each encounter, he looked for ways to enrich their lives.

His message remained constant: God is a loving Father, and every person is his child. His method was equally consistent—he asked questions until people began asking him questions in return. He listened far more than he spoke, and those he helped most often heard the fewest words from him.

The people who gained the most were those carrying heavy burdens —the anxious, the defeated, the overwhelmed. Jesus gave them something rare: complete attention. He listened without judgment as they poured out their troubles. Then he offered practical suggestions for their immediate problems while also speaking words of comfort. And always, in whatever way suited each person, he helped them understand that they were children of a God who loved them.

During his six months in Rome, Jesus had meaningful contact with more than five hundred people. He considered it one of the richest periods of his life.

He talked politics with a Roman senator, and the conversation so affected the man that he spent years trying to change imperial policy —arguing that the people should support the government rather than the government feeding the people.

He dined with a wealthy slaveholder named Claudius and spoke about human dignity and divine sonship. The next morning, Claudius freed one hundred and seventeen slaves.

He counseled a Greek physician, explaining that patients have minds and souls as well as bodies. The doctor transformed his practice accordingly.

He visited nearly every part of the city. The only place he refused to go was the public baths—the sexual conduct there violated his standards.

To a Roman soldier walking beside the Tiber, he said: "Be brave of heart as well as of hand. Dare to do justice and be big enough to show mercy. Compel your lower nature to obey your higher nature as you obey your superiors. Revere goodness and exalt truth. Choose the beautiful in place of the ugly. Love your fellows and reach out for God with a whole heart, for God is your Father in heaven."

To an orator at the forum, he said: "Your eloquence is pleasing, your logic is admirable, your voice is pleasant, but your teaching is hardly true. If you could only enjoy the inspiring satisfaction of knowing God as your spiritual Father, then you might employ your powers of speech to liberate your fellows from the bondage of darkness and from the slavery of ignorance."

This orator's name was Marcus. Years later, he heard Peter preach and became a believer. When Peter was martyred, Marcus defied the Roman persecutors and continued proclaiming the gospel.

One day Jesus encountered a poor man who had been wrongly accused. He accompanied the man to court and, receiving permission to speak on his behalf, delivered an address that silenced the room:

"Justice makes a nation great, and the greater a nation the more solicitous will it be to see that injustice shall not befall even its most humble citizen. Woe upon any nation when only those who possess money and influence can secure ready justice before its courts! It is the sacred duty of a magistrate to acquit the innocent as well as to punish the guilty. Upon the impartiality, fairness, and integrity of its courts the endurance of a nation depends. Civil government is founded on justice, even as true religion is founded on mercy."

The judge reconsidered the evidence and released the prisoner. Of all Jesus's activities in Rome, this came closest to a public appearance.

A wealthy Roman Stoic, introduced by Angamon, became fascinated by Jesus's teaching. After many conversations, he asked directly: what would Jesus do with wealth if he possessed it?

Jesus answered: "I would bestow material wealth for the enhancement of material life, even as I would minister knowledge, wisdom, and spiritual service for the enrichment of the intellectual life, the ennoblement of the social life, and the advancement of the spiritual life. I would administer material wealth as a wise and effective trustee of the resources of one generation for the benefit and ennoblement of the next and succeeding generations."

The man pressed further: "What do you think a man in my position should do with his wealth? Should I keep it, or should I give it away?"

Jesus recognized genuine seeking behind the question. He said: "My good friend, I discern that you are a sincere seeker after wisdom and an honest lover of truth; therefore I am minded to lay before you my view of the solution of your problems having to do with the responsibilities of wealth."

He then offered detailed guidance on managing different types of riches. Inherited wealth carried obligations to represent past generations honestly. Discovered wealth—resources extracted from nature—should benefit as many people as possible. Profits from legitimate trade were honorable. But wealth gained through exploitation or enslavement was morally corrupt.

When doubt arose about the justice of any financial situation, Jesus counseled: "Let your decisions favor those who are in need, favor those who suffer the misfortune of undeserved hardships."

The wealthy Roman rose from his couch and declared: "My good friend, I perceive you are a man of great wisdom and goodness, and tomorrow I will begin the administration of all my wealth in accordance with your counsel."

One afternoon, Jesus and Ganid found a small boy crying in the streets. He had wandered away from home and couldn't find his way back. They were on their way to the libraries, but they set aside their plans and spent hours helping the child. Eventually they located his home and restored him to his frantic mother.

Walking away afterward, Jesus said: "You know, Ganid, most human beings are like the lost child. They spend much of their time crying in fear and suffering in sorrow when, in very truth, they are but a short distance from safety and security, even as this child was only a little way from home. And all those who know the way of truth and enjoy the assurance of knowing God should esteem it a privilege, not a duty, to offer guidance to their fellows in their efforts to find the satisfactions of living. Did we not supremely enjoy this ministry of restoring the child to his mother? So do those who lead men to God experience the supreme satisfaction of human service."

Ganid never forgot those words. For the rest of his life, he looked for lost children—literal and figurative—and helped them find their way home.

They also discovered a widow whose husband had died in an accident, leaving her with five children and no income. The situation resonated deeply with Jesus, who had lost his own father the same way. He and Ganid visited repeatedly, bringing food and clothing purchased with money Ganid obtained from his father. They didn't stop until they had found work for the eldest son so the family could support itself.

That evening, Gonod listened to his son describe their efforts. He smiled and said to Jesus: "I propose to make a scholar or a businessman of my son, and now you start out to make a philosopher or philanthropist of him."

Jesus replied: "Perhaps we will make him all four; then can he enjoy a fourfold satisfaction in life as his ear for the recognition of human melody will be able to recognize four tones instead of one."

Gonod considered this, then said: "I perceive that you really are a philosopher. You must write a book for future generations."

Jesus answered quietly: "Not a book—my mission is to live a life in this generation and for all generations. I—" He stopped himself, then turned to Ganid. "My son, it is time to retire."[1]

16

THE GREEK WORLD

Jesus left Rome as quietly as he had arrived. He said no goodbyes, made no announcements, simply departed one day with Gonod and Ganid. For a year afterward, those who had known him watched for his return. When he never reappeared, small groups began meeting informally—Stoics, Cynics, and mystery cultists drawn together by shared memories and a common fascination with his teachings. These gatherings continued until the first Christian preachers arrived in Rome and gave them a name for what they had been seeking.

The three travelers had accumulated so many purchases in Alexandria and Rome that they sent their belongings ahead by pack train. They themselves walked the Appian Way toward Tarentum, enjoying the Italian countryside and the diverse humanity that traveled this famous road.

One afternoon, resting beside the road, Ganid asked about the caste system of his native India. He had been thinking about it ever since watching Jesus treat beggars and senators with equal respect.

Jesus replied: "Though human beings differ in many ways, one from another, before God and in the spiritual world all mortals stand on an equal footing. There are only two groups of mortals in the eyes of God: those who desire to do his will and those who do not. Mankind can appropriately be divided into many classes in accordance with differing qualifications—physical, mental, social, vocational, or moral —but as these different classes of mortals appear before the judgment bar of God, they stand on an equal footing. God is truly no respecter of persons. Although you cannot escape the recognition of differential human abilities and endowments in matters intellectual, social, and moral, you should make no such distinctions in the spiritual brother-hood of men when assembled for worship in the presence of God."

Near Tarentum, they witnessed a larger boy beating a smaller one by the roadside. Jesus moved quickly, pulling the victim free and holding the aggressor at arm's length until the younger boy could escape.

The moment Jesus released his grip, Ganid launched himself at the bully and began pummeling him. Jesus immediately pulled Ganid back, allowing the frightened attacker to flee.

Ganid was indignant. "I cannot understand you, Teacher! If mercy requires that you rescue the smaller lad, does not justice demand the punishment of the larger and offending youth?"

Jesus answered patiently: "Ganid, it is true, you do not understand. Mercy ministry is always the work of the individual, but justice punishment is the function of the social, governmental, or universe administrative groups. As an individual I am beholden to show mercy; I must go to the rescue of the assaulted lad, and in all consistency I may employ sufficient force to restrain the aggressor. And that is just what I did. I achieved the deliverance of the assaulted lad; that was the end of mercy ministry. Then I forcibly detained the aggressor a suffi-cient length of time to enable the weaker party to make his escape, after which I withdrew from the affair."

He continued: "I did not proceed to sit in judgment on the aggressor, thus to pass upon his motive—to adjudicate all that entered into his attack upon his fellow—and then undertake to execute the punishment which my mind might dictate as just recompense for his wrongdoing. Ganid, mercy may be lavish, but justice is precise. Cannot you discern that no two persons are likely to agree as to the punishment which would satisfy the demands of justice? One would impose forty lashes, another twenty, while still another would advise solitary confinement. Can you not see that on this world such responsibilities had better rest upon the group or be administered by chosen representatives of the group? In civilized society and in an organized universe, the administration of justice presupposes the passing of a just sentence consequent upon fair judgment, and such prerogatives are vested in the juridical groups of the worlds."

They discussed the question for days afterward. Ganid began to understand why Jesus avoided personal combat, but one question still troubled him.

"But, Teacher, if a stronger and ill-tempered creature should attack you and threaten to destroy you, what would you do? Would you make no effort to defend yourself?"

Jesus said: "Ganid, I can well understand how some of these problems perplex you, and I will endeavor to answer your question. First, in all attacks which might be made upon my person, I would determine whether or not the aggressor was a son of God—my brother in the flesh—and if I thought such a creature did not possess moral judgment and spiritual reason, I would unhesitatingly defend myself to the full capacity of my powers of resistance. But I would not thus assault a fellow man of sonship status, even in self-defense. I would by every possible means seek to prevent and dissuade him from making such an attack and to mitigate it in case of my failure to stop it."

Then he added quietly: "Ganid, I have absolute confidence in my heavenly Father's overcare; I am consecrated to doing the will of my Father in heaven. I do not believe that real harm can befall me; I do not believe that my lifework can really be jeopardized by anything my enemies might wish to visit upon me. I am absolutely assured that the entire universe is friendly to me—this all-powerful truth I insist on believing with a wholehearted trust in spite of all appearances to the contrary."

Ganid thought about this, remembering the story of Jacob the stone mason's son who had defended Jesus in childhood. Suddenly something clicked into place.

"Oh, I begin to see! In the first place very seldom would any normal human being want to attack such a kindly person as you, and even if anyone should be so unthinking as to do such a thing, there is pretty sure to be near at hand some other mortal who will fly to your assistance. I presume you are fairly safe in your journey through life since you spend much of your time helping others and ministering to your fellows in distress—well, most likely there'll always be someone on hand to defend you."

Jesus smiled, but his eyes held something deeper. "That test has not yet come, Ganid, and when it does, we will have to abide by the Father's will."

At the Tarentum docks, waiting for their ship to finish unloading, they witnessed a man striking his wife in public. Jesus walked up behind the angry husband and tapped him gently on the shoulder.

"My friend, may I speak with you in private for a moment?"

The man was caught off guard. "Er—why—yes, what do you want with me?"

Jesus led him aside and spoke quietly: "My friend, I perceive that something terrible must have happened to you; I very much desire that you tell me what could happen to such a strong man to lead him to attack his wife, the mother of his children, and that right out here before all eyes. I am sure you must feel that you have some good reason for this assault. What did the woman do to deserve such treatment from her husband? As I look upon you, I think I discern in your face the love of justice if not the desire to show mercy. I venture to say that, if you found me out by the wayside attacked by robbers, you would unhesitatingly rush to my rescue. I dare say you have done many such brave things in the course of your life. Now, my friend, tell me what is the matter? Did the woman do something wrong, or did you foolishly lose your head and thoughtlessly assault her?"

The kindness in Jesus's face accomplished what confrontation never could. The man's anger drained away.

"I perceive you are a priest of the Cynics, and I am thankful you restrained me. My wife has done no great wrong; she is a good woman, but she irritates me by the manner in which she picks on me in public, and I lose my temper. I am sorry for my lack of self-control, and I promise to try to live up to my former pledge to one of your brothers who taught me the better way many years ago. I promise you."

Jesus said: "My brother, always remember that man has no rightful authority over woman unless the woman has willingly and voluntarily given him such authority. Your wife has engaged to go through life with you, to help you fight its battles, and to assume the far greater share of the burden of bearing and rearing your children; and in return for this special service it is only fair that she receive from you that special protection which man can give to woman as the partner who must carry, bear, and nurture the children. The loving care and consideration which a man is willing to bestow upon his wife and their children are the measure of that man's attainment of the higher levels of creative and spiritual self-consciousness. Do you not know that men and women are partners with God in that they cooperate to create beings who grow up to possess themselves of the potential of immortal souls? The Father in heaven treats the Spirit Mother of the children of the universe as one equal to himself. It is Godlike to share your life and all that relates thereto on equal terms with the mother partner who so fully shares with you that divine experience of reproducing yourselves in the lives of your children. If you can only love your children as God loves you, you will love and cherish your wife as the Father in heaven honors and exalts the mother of all the spirit children of a vast universe."

As Jesus and his companions boarded their ship, they looked back at the couple standing together on the dock, embracing through tears. Gonod, who had overheard the final part of Jesus's counsel, spent the entire voyage thinking about his own marriage. He resolved to make changes when he returned to India.

The crossing to Nicopolis was slow, the winds unfavorable. But the travelers filled the hours with conversation, reviewing their experiences in Rome and marveling at all that had happened since Jerusalem.

Ganid had caught the spirit of personal ministry. He struck up a conversation with the ship's steward, trying to share what he had learned from Jesus about God and spiritual living. When the discussion moved into deeper waters than Ganid could navigate, he called on his teacher for help.

They stayed several days in Nicopolis, the city Augustus had built to commemorate his victory at Actium. A Greek convert to Judaism named Jeramy, whom they had met aboard ship, offered them lodging. Years later, Paul would spend an entire winter in this same house with Jeramy's son during his third missionary journey.

From Nicopolis they sailed to Corinth, capital of the Roman province of Achaia.

Ganid had become genuinely interested in Jewish religion. One Sabbath, passing the synagogue and seeing people entering for services, he asked Jesus to take him inside. They heard a rabbi lecture on "The Destiny of Israel," and afterward met Crispus, the synagogue's chief ruler.

They returned many times, primarily to visit Crispus. Ganid grew fond of the entire family—Crispus, his wife, and their five children. He was fascinated by the rhythms of Jewish family life, so different from what he knew in India.

While Ganid observed domestic customs, Jesus spent hours teaching Crispus about the deeper dimensions of religious living. Over twenty conversations, he helped this thoughtful Jew see beyond ritual to relationship with God.

The seeds bore fruit years later. When Paul arrived in Corinth preaching about Jesus, the synagogue rejected his message and forbade him to speak there again. Paul turned to the gentiles—but Crispus and his entire household embraced the new faith. They became foundational supporters of the Christian community Paul established in the city.

During his eighteen months in Corinth, Paul met many others who spoke of "the Jewish tutor who traveled with the Indian merchant's son." He never discovered who this mysterious teacher had been.

Corinth drew people from across the known world. After Alexandria and Rome, it was the most cosmopolitan city in the empire—a commercial crossroads where three continents met. Ganid never tired of exploring, especially the ancient citadel that rose nearly two thousand feet above the sea.

Jesus and Ganid often visited the home of Justus, a devout Jewish merchant who lived near the synagogue. Paul would later stay in this same house, listening to Justus reminisce about the brilliant Hebrew teacher who had visited years before. Neither Paul nor Justus ever learned the teacher's true identity.

One evening, walking near where the citadel wall met the sea, they encountered two prostitutes. Ganid, knowing Jesus's high moral standards, spoke harshly to the women and waved them away.

Jesus turned to him immediately. "You mean well, but you should not presume thus to speak to the children of God, even though they chance to be his erring children. Who are we that we should sit in judgment on these women? Do you happen to know all of the circumstances which led them to resort to such methods of obtaining a livelihood? Stop here with me while we talk about these matters."

The women stood frozen, astonished that this obviously respectable man had not walked away in disgust.

In the moonlight, Jesus continued: "There lives within every human mind a divine spirit, the gift of the Father in heaven. This good spirit ever strives to lead us to God, to help us to find God and to know God; but also within mortals there are many natural physical tendencies which the Creator put there to serve the well-being of the individual and the race. Now, oftentimes, men and women become confused in their efforts to understand themselves and to grapple with the manifold difficulties of making a living in a world so largely dominated by selfishness and sin."

He looked at the women with unmistakable compassion. "I perceive, Ganid, that neither of these women is willfully wicked. I can tell by their faces that they have experienced much sorrow; they have suffered much at the hands of an apparently cruel fate; they have not intentionally chosen this sort of life; they have, in discouragement bordering on despair, surrendered to the pressure of the hour and accepted this distasteful means of obtaining a livelihood as the best way out of a situation that to them appeared hopeless. Ganid, some people are really wicked at heart; they deliberately choose to do mean things. But, tell me, as you look into these now tear-stained faces, do you see anything bad or wicked?"

Ganid's voice caught. "No, Teacher, I do not. And I apologize for my rudeness to them—I crave their forgiveness."

Jesus said: "And I bespeak for them that they have forgiven you as I speak for my Father in heaven that he has forgiven them. Now all of you come with me to a friend's house where we will seek refreshment and plan for the new and better life ahead."

The women had not spoken a word. They looked at each other, then silently followed.

Martha, Justus's wife, answered the door to find Jesus and Ganid standing with two strangers at this late hour.

Jesus said: "You will forgive us for coming at this hour, but Ganid and I desire a bite to eat, and we would share it with these our new-found friends, who are also in need of nourishment; and besides all this, we come to you with the thought that you will be interested in counseling with us as to the best way to help these women get a new start in life. They can tell you their story, but I surmise they have had much trouble, and their very presence here in your house testifies how earnestly they crave to know good people, and how willingly they will embrace the opportunity to show all the world—and even the angels of heaven—what brave and noble women they can become."

When the food was set out, Jesus rose to leave. "As it is getting late, and since the young man's father will be awaiting us, we pray to be excused while we leave you here together—three women—the beloved children of the Most High. And I will pray for your spiritual guidance while you make plans for a new and better life on earth and eternal life in the great beyond."

Jesus and Ganid departed, leaving three speechless women behind them. Martha recovered first and did exactly what Jesus had hoped— she listened to their stories and helped them find a different path. The older woman died not long afterward, but died with hope. The younger found work at Justus's business and eventually became one of the first members of Corinth's Christian church.

During their two months in the city, Jesus and Ganid talked with dozens of people. More than half would later join the Christian community when missionaries arrived.

Paul had originally planned only a brief visit to Corinth. But he found the ground remarkably prepared. People spoke of a Jewish teacher who had passed through years before. And one of the Roman Cynics Jesus had befriended—a tentmaker named Aquila, now living in Corinth with his wife Priscilla after being expelled from Rome—had already embraced Paul's message. Paul moved in with them and worked at their trade while he preached.

These circumstances kept Paul in Corinth for eighteen months.

Apart from Athens with its famous academies, Corinth was the most important city in Greece. The two months Jesus spent there gave him encounters with people from every corner of the empire. He would always remember it as one of the richest stops on the entire Mediterranean journey.[1]

17

ATHENS TO CHARAX

THEY ARRIVED IN ATHENS, AND GANID COULD BARELY CONTAIN himself. This was Greece—the cultural heart of Alexander's empire, which had once stretched all the way to his homeland of India. Here stood the city that had shaped Western thought for centuries, the birthplace of democracy and philosophy, the place where Socrates had walked and Plato had taught.

Business was light, so Gonod spent most of his time accompanying Jesus and Ganid through the ancient streets. A great university still operated in Athens, and the three visitors made frequent trips to its lecture halls. Jesus and Ganid had discussed Plato extensively during their time at the museum in Alexandria, but here they stood in the very city where those ideas had first taken shape. They examined Greek sculpture and architecture wherever examples could still be found, remnants of an artistic tradition that had dazzled the ancient world.

One evening at their inn, a Greek philosopher engaged Jesus in a discussion about science. The man spoke for nearly three hours, expounding on the methods and achievements of natural philosophy. When he finally finished, Jesus responded with ideas that left everyone present astonished.

"Scientists may some day measure the energy, or force manifestations, of gravity, light, and electricity," Jesus said, "but these same scientists can never tell you what these universe phenomena are. Science deals with physical-energy activities; religion deals with eternal values. True philosophy grows out of the wisdom which does its best to correlate these quantitative and qualitative observations. There always exists the danger that the purely physical scientist may become afflicted with mathematical pride and statistical egotism, not to mention spiritual blindness."

The Greek listened intently as Jesus continued.

"Logic is valid in the material world, and mathematics is reliable when limited in its application to physical things; but neither is to be regarded as wholly dependable or infallible when applied to life problems. Life embraces phenomena which are not wholly material. Arithmetic says that, if one man could shear a sheep in ten minutes, ten men could shear it in one minute. That is sound mathematics, but it is not true, for the ten men could not so do it; they would get in one another's way so badly that the work would be greatly delayed."

Jesus paused, then offered another illustration.

"Mathematics asserts that, if one person stands for a certain unit of intellectual and moral value, ten persons would stand for ten times this value. But in dealing with human personality it would be nearer the truth to say that such a personality association is a sum equal to the square of the number of personalities concerned in the equation rather than the simple arithmetical sum. A social group of human beings in coordinated working harmony stands for a force far greater than the simple sum of its parts."

The philosopher's expression shifted from skepticism to genuine interest as Jesus addressed the relationship between facts and values.

"Quantity may be identified as a fact, thus becoming a scientific uniformity. Quality, being a matter of mind interpretation, represents an estimate of values, and must, therefore, remain an experience of the individual. When both science and religion become less dogmatic and more tolerant of criticism, philosophy will then begin to achieve unity in the intelligent comprehension of the universe."

Jesus spoke of the underlying unity that connected all things.

"There is unity in the cosmic universe if you could only discern its workings in actuality. The real universe is friendly to every child of the eternal God. The real problem is: How can the finite mind of man achieve a logical, true, and corresponding unity of thought? This universe-knowing state of mind can be had only by conceiving that the quantitative fact and the qualitative value have a common causation in the Paradise Father. Such a conception of reality yields a broader insight into the purposeful unity of universe phenomena; it even reveals a spiritual goal of progressive personality achievement. And this is a concept of unity which can sense the unchanging background of a living universe of continually changing impersonal relations and evolving personal relationships."

He concluded by addressing the fundamental nature of reality itself.

"Matter and spirit and the state intervening between them are three interrelated and interassociated levels of the true unity of the real universe. Regardless of how divergent the universe phenomena of fact and value may appear to be, they are, after all, unified in the Supreme. Reality of material existence attaches to unrecognized energy as well as to visible matter. When the energies of the universe are so slowed down that they acquire the requisite degree of motion, then, under favorable conditions, these same energies become mass. And forget not, the mind which can alone perceive the presence of apparent realities is itself also real. And the fundamental cause of this universe of energy-mass, mind, and spirit, is eternal—it exists and consists in the nature and reactions of the Universal Father and his absolute coordinates."

When Jesus finished, everyone sat in stunned silence. The Greek philosopher rose slowly to take his leave. "At last my eyes have beheld a Jew who thinks something besides racial superiority and talks something besides religion," he said. Then he departed into the night.

Their stay in Athens proved pleasant and intellectually stimulating, but Jesus found limited success in reaching people on a deeper level. Too many Athenians of that era were either puffed up with pride over their city's former glory or mentally dull—descendants of the slaves who had served earlier generations when Greece truly produced great minds. Still, Jesus managed to engage a few sharp thinkers among the citizens.

From Athens they sailed by way of Troas to Ephesus, the capital of the Roman province of Asia. The city's fame centered on the Temple of Artemis, one of the seven wonders of the ancient world. The enormous structure stood about two miles outside the city walls, and the three travelers made multiple trips to see it.

Artemis was the most celebrated goddess in all of Asia Minor, a deity whose roots stretched back to ancient Anatolian mother-goddess worship. The crude idol housed within the massive temple was said to have fallen from heaven. Ganid's early religious training in India had taught him to revere images as symbols of divine realities, and despite his travels with Jesus, old habits persisted. He purchased a small silver shrine depicting the fertility goddess as a memento.

That evening, they discussed the worship of objects fashioned by human hands. Jesus gently challenged the assumptions behind such practices, helping Ganid think more deeply about the difference between symbols and the realities they were meant to represent.

On their third day in Ephesus, they walked down to the river to watch workmen dredge the harbor entrance. At midday they fell into conversation with a young Phoenician who was clearly struggling. The man was homesick and deeply discouraged. Worse, he seethed with envy over a colleague who had received a promotion he felt should have been his.

Jesus listened with compassion, then offered comfort. He quoted an old Hebrew proverb: "A man's gift makes room for him and brings him before great men." The words seemed to ease the young man's bitterness, at least for a time.

Of all the major cities on their Mediterranean tour, Ephesus would prove least responsive to the later efforts of Christian missionaries. The faith eventually took root there through Paul's work—he would spend more than two years in the city, earning his living as a tentmaker while lecturing each night in a local philosophy school. But that chapter lay in the future.

During their stay, Jesus held several profitable conversations with a progressive Greek thinker connected to the local academy. In one of these discussions, Jesus had repeatedly used the word "soul." The philosopher finally asked what he meant by the term.

"The soul is the self-reflective, truth-discerning, and spirit-perceiving part of man which forever elevates the human being above the level of the animal world," Jesus replied. "Self-consciousness, in and of itself, is not the soul. Moral self-consciousness is true human self-realization and constitutes the foundation of the human soul, and the soul is that part of man which represents the potential survival value of human experience. Moral choice and spiritual attainment, the ability to know God and the urge to be like him, are the characteristics of the soul. The soul of man cannot exist apart from moral thinking and spiritual activity. A stagnant soul is a dying soul. But the soul of man is distinct from the divine spirit which dwells within the mind. The divine spirit arrives simultaneously with the first moral activity of the human mind, and that is the occasion of the birth of the soul."

The Greek pressed for more detail, and Jesus continued.

"The saving or losing of a soul has to do with whether or not the moral consciousness attains survival status through eternal alliance with its associated immortal spirit endowment. Salvation is the spiritualization of the self-realization of the moral consciousness, which thereby becomes possessed of survival value. All forms of soul conflict consist in the lack of harmony between the moral, or spiritual, self-consciousness and the purely intellectual self-consciousness."

Jesus then described the soul's ultimate destiny.

"The human soul, when matured, ennobled, and spiritualized, approaches the heavenly status in that it comes near to being an entity intervening between the material and the spiritual, the material self and the divine spirit. The evolving soul of a human being is difficult of description and more difficult of demonstration because it is not discoverable by the methods of either material investigation or spiritual proving. Notwithstanding the failure of both material science and spiritual standards to discover the existence of the human soul, every morally conscious mortal knows of the existence of his soul as a real and actual personal experience."

The philosopher listened in wonder. He had never encountered such precise thinking about a concept most people used carelessly.

<hr>

Soon the travelers boarded a ship bound for Cyprus, making a brief stop at the island of Rhodes along the way. The extended time on the water refreshed them. Bodies that had grown weary from constant travel found rest; spirits that had been stretched by continuous engagement recovered their equilibrium.

They arrived at Paphos with plans for genuine relaxation. The Mediterranean tour was drawing toward its close, and they wanted to enjoy these final weeks without the pressure of appointments or agendas. After assembling supplies, they headed into the nearby mountains with well-loaded pack animals, looking forward to fresh air and natural beauty.

For two weeks they lived simply and joyfully, hiking through mountain terrain, cooking over open fires, sleeping under stars. Then, without warning, Ganid fell desperately ill.

A violent fever seized the young man, and for two weeks he burned with heat that made him delirious. Jesus and Gonod took turns keeping vigil at his bedside. They were far from any town or doctor;

moving the boy was impossible. All they could do was nurse him where he lay and hope.

Jesus demonstrated remarkable skill in caring for the sick youth. His hands were gentle but capable, his manner calm despite the gravity of the situation. Gonod watched in amazement as his hired tutor tended Ganid with the tenderness of a father and the expertise of a trained physician. Where had a religious teacher learned such things?

Slowly, the fever broke. Ganid emerged from his illness weak but alive.

During the three weeks of convalescence that followed, Jesus spent long hours with the recovering young man. They wandered through the mountains together when Ganid felt strong enough, the boy asking questions about everything they encountered—plants, animals, weather, the behavior of light and shadow. Jesus answered each inquiry thoughtfully, turning casual observations into opportunities for deeper reflection. Gonod sometimes followed at a distance, marveling at the whole performance.

In the final week of their mountain stay, the conversations took a philosophical turn. One afternoon, Jesus and Ganid discussed the nature of the human mind for hours. Eventually, the young man posed a direct question: "Teacher, what do you mean when you say that man experiences a higher form of self-consciousness than do the higher animals?"

Jesus gathered his thoughts before responding.

"My son, I have already told you much about the mind of man and the divine spirit that lives therein, but now let me emphasize that self-consciousness is a reality. When any animal becomes self-conscious, it becomes a primitive man. Such an attainment results from a coordination of function between impersonal energy and spirit-conceiving mind, and it is this phenomenon which warrants the bestowal of an absolute focal point for the human personality, the spirit of the Father in heaven."

He continued, building his explanation carefully.

"Ideas are not simply a record of sensations; ideas are sensations plus the reflective interpretations of the personal self; and the self is more than the sum of one's sensations. There begins to be something of an approach to unity in an evolving selfhood, and that unity is derived from the indwelling presence of a part of absolute unity which spiritually activates such a self-conscious animal-origin mind."

Ganid listened intently, his mind grasping for understanding.

"No mere animal could possess a time self-consciousness," Jesus explained. "Animals possess a physiological coordination of associated sensation-recognition and memory thereof, but none experience a meaningful recognition of sensation or exhibit a purposeful association of these combined physical experiences such as is manifested in the conclusions of intelligent and reflective human interpretations. And this fact of self-conscious existence, associated with the reality of his subsequent spiritual experience, constitutes man a potential son of the universe and foreshadows his eventual attainment of the Supreme Unity of the universe."

Jesus addressed the unified nature of personhood.

"Neither is the human self merely the sum of the successive states of consciousness. Without the effective functioning of a consciousness sorter and associator there would not exist sufficient unity to warrant the designation of a selfhood. Such an ununified mind could hardly attain conscious levels of human status. If the associations of consciousness were just an accident, the minds of all men would then exhibit the uncontrolled and random associations of certain phases of mental madness."

He described the spiritual dimension of human thought.

"A human mind, built up solely out of the consciousness of physical sensations, could never attain spiritual levels; this kind of material mind would be utterly lacking in a sense of moral values and would be without a guiding sense of spiritual dominance which is so essential to achieving harmonious personality unity in time, and which is inseparable from personality survival in eternity."

Jesus spoke of the qualities that lifted human minds beyond mere biology.

"The human mind early begins to manifest qualities which are super-material; the truly reflective human intellect is not altogether bound by the limits of time. That individuals so differ in their life performances indicates, not only the varying endowments of heredity and the different influences of the environment, but also the degree of unification with the indwelling spirit of the Father which has been achieved by the self, the measure of the identification of the one with the other."

Finally, he addressed the challenge of inner harmony.

"The human mind does not well stand the conflict of double allegiance. It is a severe strain on the soul to undergo the experience of an effort to serve both good and evil. The supremely happy and efficiently unified mind is the one wholly dedicated to the doing of the will of the Father in heaven. Unresolved conflicts destroy unity and may terminate in mind disruption. But the survival character of a soul is not fostered by attempting to secure peace of mind at any price, by the surrender of noble aspirations, and by the compromise of spiritual ideals; rather is such peace attained by the stalwart assertion of the triumph of that which is true, and this victory is achieved in the overcoming of evil with the potent force of good."

Ganid absorbed these words in silence. He had emerged from his brush with death with new questions about the meaning of existence. Jesus had given him a framework for thinking about consciousness, selfhood, and spiritual reality that would stay with him for the rest of his life.

The next day they descended to Salamis and took ship for Antioch.

Antioch was the capital of Roman Syria, residence of the imperial governor and third largest city in the empire. Half a million people crowded its streets—and the city's reputation for wickedness matched its size. Open immorality flourished on a scale that shocked even worldly travelers.

Gonod had business to conduct, leaving Jesus and Ganid to explore on their own. They visited most of the city's notable sites, though Jesus declined when Gonod and Ganid went to see the notorious Grove of Daphne. The shrine's reputation for debauchery held no appeal for a man of his ideals. Such scenes were less troubling to Indians, who had encountered similar phenomena in their own culture, but they repelled Jesus's Hebrew sensibilities.

Something changed in Jesus as they approached Palestine. He grew quiet and reflective, spending less time engaging strangers and more time in private thought. He wandered the city infrequently and spoke to few people. Ganid noticed the shift and questioned his teacher repeatedly until Jesus finally explained: "This city is not far from Palestine; maybe I shall come back here sometime."

The words hung in the air, mysterious and suggestive. Jesus seemed to be looking ahead to something he could not or would not describe.

Meanwhile, Ganid had begun applying the teachings he had absorbed over two years of travel. An Indian worker in his father's Antioch operation had become difficult—disgruntled, unpleasant, seemingly beyond help. Dismissal was being discussed.

When Ganid learned of the situation, he went to his father's business and sought out his fellow countryman. They talked for a long time. Ganid discovered that the man felt mismatched with his assigned responsibilities—stuck in the wrong role, unable to use his real abilities.

Ganid shared what he had learned about the Father in heaven and expanded the man's understanding of religion in various ways. But what helped most was an old Hebrew proverb: "Whatsoever your hand finds to do, do that with all your might."

The disgruntled employee found new motivation. Ganid had become a minister of truth in his own right.

After settling their affairs and packing their luggage for the final leg of the journey, the travelers joined a camel caravan headed through Sidon and Damascus and into the desert beyond.

The desert crossing was familiar territory for these experienced travelers. When Ganid saw Jesus helping load their twenty camels and then volunteering to drive their own animal, he laughed with delight. "Teacher, is there anything that you cannot do?"

Jesus smiled. "The teacher surely is not without honor in the eyes of a diligent pupil."

And so they set forth for the ancient lands of Mesopotamia.

Jesus showed intense interest in Ur, the city where Abraham had been born millennia before. The patriarch's birthplace held deep significance for anyone steeped in Hebrew tradition. Equally fascinating were the ruins and stories surrounding Susa, the ancient Persian capital. Jesus's questions and investigations so captivated Gonod and Ganid that they extended their stay by three weeks, partly to give him more time and partly because they were still hoping to persuade him to return to India with them.

It was at Ur that Ganid engaged Jesus in a lengthy conversation about the difference between knowledge, wisdom, and truth. The distinctions mattered, Ganid was learning. Facts alone could not guide a life; something more was needed.

Jesus quoted from the Hebrew wisdom tradition: "Wisdom is the principal thing; therefore get wisdom. With all your quest for knowledge, get understanding. Exalt wisdom and she will promote you. She will bring you to honor if you will but embrace her."

Ganid treasured these words. After two years with this remarkable teacher, he had come to understand that information and insight were not the same thing—and that both fell short of living truth.

Finally the day arrived that none of them wanted to face.

They stood at the port of Charax, where a ship waited to carry Gonod and Ganid back to India. The morning sun sparkled on the water. Loading was nearly complete. There was nothing left to do but say goodbye.

All three men were brave. All three were tearful.

Ganid spoke first, his voice unsteady but determined. "Farewell, Teacher, but not forever. When I come again to Damascus, I will look for you. I love you, for I think the Father in heaven must be something like you; at least I know you are much like what you have told me about him. I will remember your teaching, but most of all, I will never forget you."

Gonod took his turn. "Farewell to a great teacher, one who has made us better and helped us to know God."

Jesus replied with quiet emotion: "Peace be upon you, and may the blessing of the Father in heaven ever abide with you."

Then he stood on the shore and watched as a small boat carried his friends out to their waiting ship. The figures grew smaller. The ship raised sail. And then they were gone.

Jesus would never see Gonod and Ganid again in this world. Nor would they ever discover that the man who later appeared as Jesus of Nazareth was the same person they had known as Joshua—their teacher, their friend, their guide to God.

In India, Ganid grew into an influential man, a worthy successor to his distinguished father. Throughout his life, he spread the noble truths he had learned during those years of travel. Later, when he heard reports of a remarkable teacher in Palestine who had been crucified, Ganid recognized similarities between this "Son of Man" gospel and the teachings of his old Jewish tutor.

But it never occurred to him that Joshua and Jesus were the same person.

Thus ended the chapter in the Son of Man's life that might be called "the mission of Joshua the teacher."[1]

18

MOUNT HERMON

Throughout his Mediterranean journey, Jesus had carefully observed the peoples and cultures he encountered. Now, as he made his way back toward Palestine, he reached a final decision about the remainder of his life on earth. He had considered the matter thoroughly and concluded that his native land—the place where he had entered the world as a helpless infant—would also be where he would complete his mission. Palestine, with its mix of Jews and Gentiles, its location at the crossroads of the Roman world, would serve as the stage for the closing chapters of his earthly career.

For the first time, he felt fully satisfied with this plan. He would openly manifest his true nature and reveal his divine identity among the people of his father Joseph's homeland. The decision was entirely his own.

After bidding farewell to Gonod and Ganid at Charax in December, Jesus traveled by way of Ur to Babylon, where he joined a desert caravan heading for Damascus. From there he continued to Nazareth, pausing briefly in Capernaum to visit Zebedee's family. His brother James had taken over Jesus's former position in the boat shop, and Jesus found him there working. Jude happened to be in town as well, giving the brothers a chance to talk.

During this stop, Jesus completed a piece of unfinished business. John Zebedee had managed to purchase a small house, and Jesus now transferred ownership of it to James. This would soon prove significant.

The Mediterranean journey had provided Jesus with enough money to live on until his public ministry began. But apart from the Zebedee family and the people he had met during his extraordinary travels, no one knew where he had actually been. His family believed he had spent the time studying in Alexandria. Jesus never confirmed this assumption, but neither did he openly correct it.

He spent several weeks in Nazareth visiting with family and friends. He put in some time at the repair shop with his brother Joseph, but devoted most of his attention to Mary and Ruth. Ruth was nearly fifteen now—a young woman—and this was Jesus's first real opportunity to have extended conversations with her since she had grown up.

Simon and Jude had both wanted to marry for some time, but they had been waiting for Jesus's blessing. Though James functioned as head of the family in most practical matters, the brothers still wanted their eldest sibling's approval for something as significant as marriage. Now that Jesus had returned, Simon and Jude could finally proceed. The double wedding took place in early March. All the older children were now married; only Ruth remained at home with Mary.

Jesus visited individually with each family member in his usual warm manner. But when they gathered as a group, he had remarkably little to say. They noticed this among themselves and wondered about it. Mary found her firstborn son's behavior peculiarly distant.

Around the time Jesus was preparing to leave, an opportunity presented itself. A large caravan passing through Nazareth lost its conductor to sudden illness. Jesus, with his gift for languages and his travel experience, volunteered to take the man's place. The position would require a year's absence.

Since all his brothers were now married and his mother was living with Ruth, Jesus called a family conference. He proposed that Mary and Ruth move to Capernaum and live in the house he had recently given to James. They agreed. A few days after Jesus departed with the caravan, Mary and Ruth relocated to Capernaum, where Mary would spend the rest of her life. Joseph and his family moved into the old Nazareth home.

On the first of April, Jesus left Nazareth as conductor of a caravan bound for the Caspian Sea region. The route took them from Jerusalem through Damascus, past Lake Urmia, and across Assyria, Media, and Parthia to the southeastern shores of the Caspian. A full year would pass before he returned.

This journey became another adventure in exploration and personal ministry. Jesus developed meaningful relationships with the passengers, guards, and camel drivers in his caravan family. Scores of people living along their route emerged from encounters with this unusual caravan conductor with richer, fuller lives. Not everyone who met him was transformed, but the vast majority of those who talked with him became better people for the rest of their days.

Of all his travels, this trip carried Jesus closest to the Orient and deepened his understanding of Far Eastern peoples. He made personal contact with representatives of virtually every surviving race on earth except the red. Europeans from the distant West and Asians from the Far East alike listened to his words about hope and eternal life. All were receptive to the living truth he shared, regardless of their background.

The caravan succeeded in every practical way as well. Jesus functioned as an executive, responsible for the goods entrusted to his care and the safety of all travelers in the party. He discharged these duties faithfully, efficiently, and wisely—a most interesting episode in his human experience.

On the return journey, Jesus left the caravan at Lake Urmia, where he stayed for more than two weeks. He then traveled back to Damascus as a passenger with a later caravan. The camel owners tried to persuade him to remain in their employ, but he declined and continued on to Capernaum, arriving in early April of the following year. Nazareth was no longer his home. From this point forward, Capernaum would be where Jesus belonged—though he never again lived with his family. When in town, he stayed with the Zebedees.

During his stopover at Lake Urmia, Jesus encountered something remarkable. On one of the islands near the western shore stood an unusual building—a lecture amphitheater dedicated to what its founders called "the spirit of religion." It was essentially a temple devoted to the philosophy of religions.

A wealthy merchant named Cymboyton had built this institution with his three sons. The family traced their ancestry through many diverse peoples, and their vision reflected that cosmopolitan heritage. The school operated daily: lectures and discussions began at ten in the morning, afternoon sessions started at three, and evening debates opened at eight. Cymboyton or one of his sons always presided.

More than thirty religions and religious movements were represented on the faculty. Teachers were chosen, supported, and accredited by their respective religious groups. About seventy-five instructors lived on the island in small cottages, with group assignments rotated monthly by lot. Anyone who displayed intolerance or a contentious spirit faced immediate dismissal; an alternate would be installed in his place without ceremony.

The teachers worked to demonstrate how similar their various religions were regarding the fundamental questions of existence. Only one doctrine was required for admission to the faculty: each teacher had to represent a religion that recognized God—some form of supreme Deity. Five independent teachers served who belonged to no organized religion at all. Jesus appeared before them as such an independent teacher.

On his initial visit, Jesus participated in several discussions. Cymboyton was so impressed that he arranged for Jesus to return on his way back from the Caspian and deliver a formal series of lectures. Jesus agreed. Upon his return, he gave twenty-four lectures on "The Brotherhood of Men" and conducted twelve evening sessions of questions, discussions, and debates.

This became the most systematic and formal teaching Jesus ever delivered. Never before or after did he say so much on a single subject. In reality, his lectures addressed two interconnected themes: the kingdom of God and the kingdoms of men.

The core of Jesus's teaching at Urmia concerned the relationship between divine sovereignty and human brotherhood.

The brotherhood of men, he explained, is founded on the fatherhood of God. The family of God derives from the love of God—for God is love. The Father divinely loves all his children.

The kingdom of heaven—the divine government—rests on the fact of divine sovereignty. Since God is spirit, this kingdom is spiritual. It represents a spiritual relationship between God and humanity, not a material or merely intellectual arrangement.

Religious peace and brotherhood can exist only when all religions willingly set aside claims of exclusive authority. When different faiths recognize the spirit sovereignty of God the Father, they can remain at peace with one another. But the moment one religion assumes superiority over all others—claiming exclusive spiritual authority—it will become intolerant and even persecutory.

God gives a fragment of his spirit self to dwell in the heart of every person. Spiritually, all people are equal. The kingdom of heaven knows no castes, classes, social levels, or economic divisions. All are brothers and sisters.

The Urmia community succeeded because its members had surrendered all notions of religious sovereignty. Spiritually, they believed in a sovereign God. Socially, they accepted Cymboyton's authority without challenge. Everyone understood what would happen to any teacher who tried to dominate his colleagues.

Lasting religious peace on earth, Jesus taught, requires that all religious groups freely surrender their notions of divine favor, chosen-people status, and spiritual sovereignty. Only when God the Father becomes supreme in human hearts will people become true religious brothers, living together in genuine peace.

Jesus also addressed political sovereignty—though his teachings on this subject were later adapted by those who recorded them to speak more directly to conditions far beyond his own time.

In Jesus's era, only two great world powers existed: the Roman Empire in the West and the Han Empire in the East, separated by the Parthian kingdom and the lands around the Caspian. The political landscape of later centuries would grow vastly more complex.

The essential principle remained constant: war on earth will never end as long as nations cling to illusions of unlimited sovereignty. Only two levels of sovereignty ultimately matter—the spiritual free will of individual persons and the collective sovereignty of all humanity. Everything in between is relative and temporary, valuable only insofar as it serves the welfare of individuals and the whole human race.

As political organizations grow larger, minor conflicts between smaller groups decrease—but the potential for catastrophic wars increases. When great powers wielding massive sovereignty come into contact, the stage is set for devastating global conflicts.

The difficulty in evolving from family-level organization to world government lies in the resistance of intermediate levels. Families sometimes defy clans; clans and tribes resist territorial states; states resist larger unifications. Each new level of political development is hindered by loyalties formed at earlier stages. The same patriotism that enables nations to form also makes broader unity difficult to achieve.

Peace will come to earth only when nations intelligently and fully surrender their sovereign powers to a government representing all humanity. International organizations and leagues of nations represent steps in the right direction—they can prevent minor wars and control smaller nations—but they cannot prevent world wars or restrain the most powerful governments. As long as nations remain infected with the virus of absolute sovereignty, they will go to war.

The creation of genuine world government would not diminish individual freedom—it would enhance it. Citizens of great powers today are taxed, regulated, and controlled in ways that would largely disappear if national governments surrendered their sovereignty over international affairs to a global authority. True collective security requires that the collective include all humanity.

After his return from the Caspian journey, Jesus knew his world travels were essentially complete. He would make only one more trip outside Palestine—into Syria.

Following a brief visit to Capernaum, he went to Nazareth for a few days, then continued north to Tyre and Sidon, destined for Antioch.

Jesus spent more than two months in Antioch, longer than anywhere else on this journey. He worked, observed, studied, visited, and ministered—learning how people lived, thought, felt, and responded to their circumstances. For three weeks he earned his living as a tentmaker.

From Antioch, Jesus traveled south along the coast to Caesarea, then continued to Joppa. He journeyed inland through Jamnia, Ashdod, and Gaza, then took the trail to Beersheba, where he stayed for a week.

Then began his final tour as a private individual through the heart of Palestine. From Beersheba in the south to Dan in the north, he walked through the land of his ancestors. He stopped at Hebron and Bethlehem, where he saw his birthplace. He passed through Jerusalem without visiting Bethany. He continued through Beeroth, Lebonah, Sychar, Shechem, and Samaria. Through Geba, En-Gannim, Endor, and Madon he traveled. Past Magdala and Capernaum he journeyed, then east of the Waters of Merom until he reached Caesarea Philippi, near the ancient city of Dan.

Throughout this year, Jesus was known by different names in different regions: the carpenter of Nazareth, the boatbuilder of Capernaum, the scribe of Damascus, the teacher of Alexandria.

Something within him—the divine spirit that had dwelt in his mind since childhood—now led Jesus to leave behind the places where people gathered. He would ascend Mount Hermon to finish mastering his human mind and complete his full consecration to the work that lay ahead.

This would be one of the most extraordinary periods in his entire earthly existence. Another similar experience awaited him later, in the hills near Pella after his baptism. But this time on Mount Hermon marked the end of his purely human career—the technical completion of his mortal life—while the later isolation would begin a more divine phase.

Near the middle of August, Jesus established a base camp in the village of Beit Jenn, in the foothills of Hermon. He secured supplies and hired a local boy named Tiglath to assist him. Together they climbed to a point about six thousand feet above sea level, where they built a stone container. Tiglath would deposit food there twice weekly.

On that first day, after leaving the boy behind, Jesus paused to pray. Among other things, he asked his Father to send his seraphic guardian back to watch over Tiglath. He requested permission to face his final struggle alone. The request was granted. He would go forward with only his indwelling divine spirit to guide and sustain him.

Jesus ate sparingly on the mountain, fasting completely only a day or two at a time. The celestial being he encountered there—the adversary he wrestled with in spirit and defeated in power—was real. It was one of his erring sons who rebelled against their father's divine authority and corrupted this corner of the universe. It was not a phantom conjured by a weakened, starving mind that could no longer distinguish reality from delusion.

For six weeks—the last three weeks of August and the first three of September—Jesus lived in unbroken communion with his heavenly Father. During this time, he completed the mortal task of achieving full circles of mind-understanding and personality-control. His indwelling spirit completed its assigned services. The mortal goal of this earth creature was attained. Only the final harmony between his human mind and divine spirit remained to be consummated.

After more than five weeks of this communion, Jesus became absolutely certain of his nature and the inevitability of his triumph. He fully believed in—and did not hesitate to assert—the supremacy of his divine nature over his human nature.

Near the end of his mountain sojourn, Jesus asked his Father for permission to hold conference with his adversary—to face him as the Son of Man, as Joshua ben Joseph. The request was granted.

During the final week on Mount Hermon, the great temptation

occurred—the universe trial. Satan, representing Lucifer, was present and made fully visible to him.

This temptation had nothing to do with food after fasting. It had nothing to do with temple pinnacles or presumptuous stunts. It had nothing to do with the kingdoms of this world. It concerned the sovereignty of a mighty and glorious universe. The symbolic stories recorded later were for a humanity that thought in simpler terms. The actual struggle was far more profound.

To the many proposals and counterproposals from the emissary of rebellion, Jesus gave only one reply: "May the will of my Paradise Father prevail, and you, my rebellious son, may the Ancients of Days judge you divinely. I am your Creator-father; I can hardly judge you justly, and my mercy you have already spurned. I commit you to the adjudication of the Judges of a greater universe."

To every compromise and counterfeit suggestion, to every specious proposal about how he might conduct his mission, Jesus responded simply: "The will of my Father in Paradise be done."

When the ordeal ended, his guardian angel returned and ministered to him.

On an afternoon in late summer, amid the trees and silence of nature, Jesus won the unquestioned sovereignty of his universe. On that day, he completed the task set for himself—to live fully the incarnated life in mortal flesh on an evolutionary world. The announcement of this achievement would not come until his baptism months later, but the victory was won on that mountain.

When Jesus descended from Mount Hermon, the cosmic insurrection that had plagued his domain was virtually settled. He had paid the final price required to attain universal sovereignty, which now empowered him to deal with any future upheavals swiftly and decisively. The so-called "great temptation" actually occurred here, before his baptism—not in the wilderness afterward.

At the end of his sojourn, Jesus met Tiglath coming up the mountain with food. He turned the boy back with only these words: "The period of rest is over; I must return to my Father's business."

He was a silent and profoundly changed man as they journeyed back to Dan. There he parted with Tiglath, giving him the donkey as a gift, and proceeded south to Capernaum by the same route he had come.

<hr>

Summer was ending. Jesus attended a family gathering in Capernaum over the Sabbath, then started for Jerusalem with John Zebedee. They traveled east of the lake, through Gerasa, and down the Jordan valley. John noticed a great change in his companion but could not fully understand it.

They stopped overnight at Bethany with Lazarus and his sisters before entering Jerusalem early the next morning. They spent nearly three weeks in and around the city. John explored Jerusalem while Jesus walked the surrounding hills, engaging in long seasons of spiritual communion with his Father.

Both attended the solemn observances of the Day of Atonement. John was deeply impressed by the ceremonies of this most sacred day in Jewish religious life. But Jesus remained a thoughtful, silent spectator. To him, the elaborate rituals were pitiful and pathetic—misrepresentations of his Father's character. He saw them as a travesty upon divine justice and infinite mercy. He burned to proclaim the real truth about his Father's loving nature, but his inner guide cautioned him: the hour had not yet come.

That night at Bethany, Jesus let slip several remarks that disturbed John. The young man never fully grasped what his friend was trying to say.

Jesus planned to stay through the Feast of Tabernacles—the annual holiday of all Palestine, the Jewish vacation time. Though he did not participate in the festivities, he clearly enjoyed watching others celebrate. The lighthearted joy of young and old alike gave him pleasure.

Midway through the festival week, Jesus told John he wanted to retire to the hills for communion with his Father. John offered to accompany him, but Jesus insisted he stay and enjoy the celebrations. "It is not required of you to bear the burden of the Son of Man," he said. "Only the watchman must keep vigil while the city sleeps in peace."

Jesus did not return to Jerusalem. After nearly a week alone in the hills near Bethany, he departed for Capernaum. On the way home, he spent a day and night on the slopes of Mount Gilboa, near where King Saul had taken his own life centuries before. When he finally reached Capernaum, he seemed more cheerful than when he had left John in Jerusalem.

<hr>

The next morning, Jesus went to the chest containing his personal belongings in Zebedee's workshop. He put on his work apron and presented himself for duty. "It behooves me to keep busy while I wait for my hour to come," he explained.

He worked in the boatshop for several months—through the autumn and into January of the following year—alongside his brother James. Whatever doubts later arose to trouble James's understanding of Jesus's mission, this period of working together strengthened a faith he would never entirely abandon.

During these final months as a craftsman, Jesus focused on the interior finishing of larger vessels. He took great care with his work, experiencing genuine satisfaction when he completed something well. He wasted no time on trivialities but was meticulous about essentials.

As time passed, rumors reached Capernaum about a man named John who was preaching and baptizing penitents in the Jordan. "The kingdom of heaven is at hand," John proclaimed. "Repent and be baptized."

Jesus listened to these reports as John slowly worked his way up the Jordan valley from the ford nearest Jerusalem. But Jesus continued making boats. He waited as John gradually approached, passing through village after village, until finally, in January, he reached a point near Pella.

Jesus intended to present himself to John for baptism.

A great transformation had been taking place within Jesus over many years. Few who had known him during his travels—who had enjoyed his visits and benefited from his personal ministry—would have recognized him as the public teacher he was about to become. The quiet, helpful stranger who had touched their lives seemed a different person from the authoritative figure who would soon emerge.

This change of mind and spirit had been progressing for a long time. It was completed during those eventful weeks on Mount Hermon.

The private man was ready to become public.[1]

19

THE VOICE IN THE WILDERNESS

For fifteen months, the voice of John the Baptist thundered across the Jordan valley, and all of Palestine listened.

He had emerged from the Judean wilderness in March of A.D. 25—a striking figure in camel's hair and leather belt, deliberately evoking the prophet Elijah. At thirty, John stood over six feet tall, with flowing hair and eyes that seemed to look straight through those who heard him. His message was direct: "Repent, for the kingdom of heaven is at hand!"

The timing could not have been more potent. For a century, the Jewish people had languished under foreign rule, wrestling with an agonizing theological puzzle. Their scriptures taught that righteousness brought prosperity and power. Yet here they were—God's chosen people—subjugated first by Greeks, now by Romans. Where was the promised deliverance? Where was the Messiah who would restore the throne of David?

Into this charged atmosphere came John, preaching at the ancient ford near Jericho—where Joshua had led the Israelites into the promised land centuries earlier. The location seemed prophetic. And his message electrified the nation: the wait was nearly over. The kingdom was coming. Prepare yourselves.

What distinguished John from other preachers was baptism. Ritual washing was familiar to Jews, but it had always been reserved for gentile converts. Now John required Jews themselves to submit—a stunning demand implying that even God's chosen people needed cleansing before the coming kingdom. Tens of thousands responded, wading into the Jordan to be immersed by this strange, compelling prophet.

Delegations arrived from Jerusalem—priests and Levites demanding to know his authority and whether he claimed to be the Messiah. John denied it directly. Not the Messiah. Not Elijah returned. Not the prophet Moses promised. He was merely a voice crying in the wilderness, preparing the way for one far greater—one whose sandals he was unworthy to touch. He baptized with water; the coming one would baptize with the Holy Spirit.

The crowds pressed closer. Who was this coming one? When would he appear?

John himself wondered. His mother Elizabeth had told him all his life that his cousin Jesus of Nazareth was destined for greatness—that angels had announced both their births, that Jesus was somehow the promised deliverer. But Jesus had lived quietly in Galilee for thirty years, working as a carpenter and a boatbuilder, showing no signs of claiming any special role. John had last seen him years earlier, and that conversation had only deepened the mystery. Jesus spoke of spiritual realities that didn't align with John's understanding of the Messiah. He counseled patience—waiting for "the Father's hour."

So John preached and baptized, drawing larger crowds, moving gradually up the Jordan valley. By December of A.D. 25 he had reached the region near Pella, and his fame had spread across Palestine. In Capernaum, where Jesus now lived with the Zebedee family, people talked of little else.

Jesus had been watching, waiting, listening for the inner signal that his time had come. The previous summer he had spent six weeks alone on Mount Hermon, wrestling with the full weight of his identity and mission. He emerged from that mountain retreat triumphant. His human mind had reached perfect harmony with his divine mind. The long preparation was complete.

Now, as reports reached Capernaum that John had moved north toward Pella, Jesus sensed the hour approaching. His brothers James and Jude had talked of going to hear John preach, perhaps even to be baptized. On Saturday evening, January 12, A.D. 26, they raised the subject again after the synagogue services.

Jesus asked them to wait until the next day for his answer. That night he slept little, communing with his Father, seeking final confirmation of what he already knew. The time had come to step from obscurity and begin the work for which he had been born—and for which, in ways beyond human comprehension, he had existed before all worlds.

The next morning, Sunday, Jesus worked at his bench in Zebedee's boat shop as usual. James and Jude arrived at noon with food, waiting in the lumber room for his answer. Just before the midday break, Jesus laid down his tools, removed his apron, and went out to meet them.

"My hour has come," he said. "Let us go to John."

They left immediately, eating lunch as they walked, taking the road down toward the Jordan valley. They stayed overnight near Jericho and reached John's baptizing site around noon the next day—Monday, January 14, A.D. 26.

The scene at the river was remarkable. Hundreds lined the banks, waiting their turn. John stood waist-deep in the water, his powerful voice carrying across the crowd as he immersed each penitent. His disciples moved among the people—answering questions, organizing lines, keeping order.

Jesus and his brothers took their place in line. John was so absorbed in his work that he didn't look up as the queue advanced. Scores of repentant men and women passed through his hands, rising from the water to begin lives of renewed devotion.

Then Jesus stood before him.

John looked into the face of his cousin—unseen for years—and the ceremonies halted. "Why do you come down into the water to greet me?" he asked.

"To be subject to your baptism," Jesus answered.

"But I have need to be baptized by you. Why do you come to me?"

Jesus spoke quietly, for John's ears alone: "Bear with me now, for it becomes us to set this example for my brothers standing here with me, and that the people may know that my hour has come."

There was finality in Jesus' voice—and something more. Authority. Not the bluster of self-importance, but the calm certainty of one who knows exactly who he is and what he must do.

The baptism itself took only moments. John placed his hands on Jesus' shoulders, spoke the blessing, and lowered him beneath the Jordan's surface. He baptized Jesus' brothers James and Jude as well, then dismissed the crowd for the day, announcing he would resume at noon tomorrow.

As people departed, the four men remained in the water. Then something appeared above Jesus—a momentary manifestation that John, James, and Jude all witnessed. They heard a voice: "This is my beloved Son in whom I am well pleased." Only the four standing in the water heard the words and saw what descended.

A great change came over Jesus, a quality of settled presence, of absolute certainty. The Nazareth carpenter had stepped fully into his identity as something far greater. Rising from the water in silence, he took leave of them and walked toward the eastern hills.

John followed Jesus a short distance—long enough to tell him about Gabriel's visit to his mother before either of them was born, the story Elizabeth had repeated so many times. Jesus listened but made no reply. John watched him go. No one saw Jesus again for forty days.

In the days and weeks that followed, John's preaching took on new conviction regarding the coming kingdom and the expected Messiah. When Jesus finally returned from the wilderness, John stood on a large rock and declared: "Behold the Son of God, the deliverer of the world! This is he of whom I said, 'After me will come one preferred before me because he was before me.' For this cause I came from the wilderness to preach repentance and baptize with water, proclaiming that the kingdom of heaven is at hand. Now comes one who shall baptize you with the Holy Spirit."

For forty days Jesus had remained alone in the Perean hills, wrestling with questions that would shape the course of his ministry and the future of the world. The voice in the wilderness had done its work. Now a greater voice would begin to speak.

But for John's disciples—and for James and Jude, who had returned to Galilee burning with questions—one thing was already certain. Something unprecedented had entered the world. The kingdom that John had announced was no longer merely coming. It had arrived.[1]

THE GREAT DECISIONS

When Jesus walked east into the Perean hills after his baptism, he carried with him a burden no human being had ever borne. He was now fully conscious of his dual nature—human and divine—and of the vast responsibilities that came with it. The forty days that followed would become the most consequential period of solitary reflection in human history.

Jesus did not enter the wilderness to fast or practice self-denial. He was no ascetic, and he intended to overturn such ideas about approaching God. His purpose was different altogether: to consider the implications of his new status and make decisive choices about his coming work. This was a time for reviewing the entire trajectory of his earthly mission and developing plans for how best to serve the world through his ministry.

While searching the hills for shelter, Jesus encountered Gabriel—the same celestial messenger who had announced his birth to Mary years before. Gabriel brought word from the highest authorities: the long experience of earthly life was essentially complete. Through his perfect submission to the Father's will, Jesus had earned full authority. He was free to end his earthly life whenever he chose and return to his former glory.

This was not a temptation but an offer—and a test of a different kind. Jesus could leave. His work, technically speaking, was finished. He had lived a human life in perfect harmony with divine will, and that achievement could not be taken from him.

But Jesus did not come merely to achieve something for himself. He came to reveal the Father to humanity and to establish a new understanding of the kingdom of heaven in the hearts of men.

During this conference with Gabriel, another messenger arrived. The message was formal: The records were complete. Jesus' sovereignty stood secure. He was free, at any time and in any manner of his choosing, to end his mortal bestowal and ascend on high to receive full authority over heaven and earth. From this point forward, his course was entirely his own to determine.

Jesus received this confirmation silently. He spent extended time conversing with Gabriel about larger concerns, sent greetings to those who had commissioned his earthly mission, and assured them that in his coming work he would remain mindful of the counsel given before his incarnation.

The choice was made. He would stay. He would complete what he had come to do. But how? That was the question that consumed the remaining weeks of his isolation.

Day after day, Jesus developed his plans for public ministry. The decisions before him would shape not only his own path but the spiritual future of an entire world.

The first decision concerned his relationship to the celestial powers available to him. Vast hosts of angels stood ready to serve—awaiting his command. Should he deploy them in his work?

Jesus decided against it. He would employ none of these superhuman resources unless the Father's will clearly allowed it. He voluntarily set aside all supernatural assistance for his earthly work. He would live as a man among men, depending on human means and divine guidance rather than celestial intervention.

This decision carried enormous implications. Any supernatural elements in his ministry would come from the Father's direct action, not Jesus' initiative. He would not summon angels for protection, invoke cosmic powers to prove his authority, or circumvent natural law to ease his path.

The second decision addressed physical needs. By the third day of solitary meditation, hunger had set in. Should he use his creative powers to produce food, or seek it as any ordinary person would?

The question was not trivial. Jesus had the power to transform matter, to create sustenance from nothing. But he chose otherwise. For his personal needs, he would follow normal earthly existence. He would neither transcend nor violate natural law for his own benefit.

He expressed his conclusion in scriptural terms: "Man shall not live by bread alone but by every word that proceeds from the mouth of God." This decision about physical appetite became his final position on all bodily urges. Superhuman power might possibly serve others; for himself, never.

The third decision involved personal safety. How would he respond to danger? Sitting beneath a tree on an overhanging ledge, a precipice before him, Jesus knew he could throw himself into the void without harm—if he reversed his earlier decisions and called upon celestial protection.

Jews expected a Messiah operating above natural law. Scripture promised angels would bear up the righteous, that no harm would touch God's chosen. Would such a demonstration win over his misguided people?

Jesus concluded it would not. Such presumption—defying the Father's natural laws—would trivialize the established order rather than reveal the Father's character. He would take normal precautions for his safety but refrain from supernatural intervention when life's ultimate crisis arrived.

The fourth decision struck at the heart of messianic expectation. Should he use any of his superhuman powers to attract attention and win adherents? Should he gratify the Jewish hunger for the spectacular and the marvelous?

He decided he should not.

Jesus recognized that miracle-working would produce only external allegiance by overwhelming the material mind. Such displays would neither reveal God nor genuinely save anyone. He refused to become a wonder-worker. His single task would be establishing the kingdom of heaven in human hearts.

Jews expected a Messiah who would surpass even Moses—drawing water from rock, feeding multitudes with manna, performing signs that would compel belief. Jesus had the power to fulfill these expectations. But he saw such a course as regression toward primitive magic and degraded religious practice.

He grieved for his people. He understood how they had been conditioned to expect a Messiah bringing miraculous abundance. But he had not come to multiply bread and wine or merely to address temporal needs. He came to reveal the Father to humanity and to invite people into sincere efforts to live according to the Father's will.

The fifth decision concerned how he would present himself. Jews envisioned a deliverer arriving in power, crushing enemies, establishing them as world rulers. Jesus knew this hope would not be realized—at least not as they imagined.

He considered launching his spiritual kingdom with a brilliant display of power. The option was available to him. But he rejected it. He had won the world through submission to the Father's will, and he would finish as he had begun—as the Son of Man.

He would return to Galilee and quietly begin the proclamation of the kingdom, trusting his Father to work out the details day by day.

On his last day in isolation, before descending to rejoin John and the disciples, Jesus made his final commitment. He spoke aloud to the divine presence within: "And in all other matters, as in these decisions now recorded, I pledge to remain subject to the will of my Father."

He descended the mountain. His face shone triumphant with the radiance of spiritual victory.

The forty days were complete. Jesus of Nazareth had made the choices that would govern his entire public ministry. He would not use supernatural power for personal benefit. He would not perform wonders to compel belief. He would not compromise with evil or take shortcuts to glory. He would live as a man among men, revealing the Father through the power of his love and the truth of his teaching.

It was now late February, A.D. 26. The voice in the wilderness was still preaching. The apostles had not yet been chosen. The first miracle had not yet occurred. The Sermon on the Mount had not yet been delivered.

But the foundation had been laid. The decisions had been made. And the one who made them knew exactly what kind of ministry he would conduct—and what kind he would refuse.

The kingdom of heaven was about to begin its work on earth.[1]

EPILOGUE

THE WORLD REMEMBERS JESUS FOR THREE YEARS. THREE YEARS OF teaching, healing, gathering followers, and confronting authorities. Three years that ended on a Roman cross and an empty tomb. Those years changed history.

But thirty years came first.

Thirty years of ordinary human life — or what appeared to be ordinary. A boy growing up in a small village. A teenager suddenly responsible for a widowed mother and eight siblings. A young man working with his hands, earning wages, paying taxes, attending weddings and funerals. A craftsman whose boats became the standard on the Sea of Galilee. A traveler who walked the roads of the Roman world and sat with people from every nation and background.

These were the years that forged the man.

The patience Jesus showed with confused disciples was learned in a Nazareth carpenter shop, explaining things again and again to younger brothers who didn't always understand.

The compassion he extended to sinners and outcasts was practiced first with strangers in Mediterranean port cities. The authority with which he taught in synagogues grew from decades of study, reflection, and inner communion with his Father. The calm he maintained before Pilate and Herod was the same calm he discovered as a fourteen-year-old facing impossible responsibilities.

Nothing in his public ministry appeared from nowhere. Every quality that astonished the crowds had been quietly developed during the years no one recorded.

Consider what these hidden years reveal:

The God-man did not arrive on earth fully formed, delivering pronouncements from on high. He grew. He learned. He struggled with the same tensions every thoughtful person faces: duty versus desire, ambition versus responsibility, the call of the spirit versus the demands of the flesh. He was tested in all points as we are, yet without surrendering to selfishness or despair.

He knew hunger, exhaustion, grief, and frustration. He experienced the death of his father, the misunderstanding of his family, the rejection of a woman who loved him, and the slow years of waiting for a mission that seemed perpetually delayed. He earned calluses on his hands and dust on his feet.

And through it all, he developed an unshakeable relationship with the Father he came to reveal.

These missing years show us that the life Jesus lived was not a performance staged for our benefit but a genuine human experience embraced in its fullness. The divinity that would later blaze forth in miracles and resurrection was present all along — but it was present in a man who had learned what it meant to be human.

When his hour finally came and Jesus stood before John at the Jordan, he spoke as one with earned authority. Not earned in the sense of proving himself to God, but earned in the sense of completing the preparation. The vessel was ready. The human mind and the divine spirit had become one. The carpenter from Nazareth was prepared to become the teacher of a world.

This book, disclosing the missing years of the life of Jesus of Nazareth, is foundational. What follows in Book Two—the gathering of apostles, the public ministry, the teachings, the miracles, the mounting opposition—should make far more sense now. The Jesus who walks through those familiar scenes is no longer a mysterious figure who appeared suddenly at age thirty. He is someone we have come to know through three decades of a very human experience.

The Universe Maker became a man from Nazareth.

Now the man from Nazareth will reveal the Universe Maker.

FROM THE AUTHOR

Thank you for reading. This book is the culmination of twenty years of spiritual seeking, study, and reflection.

If you're willing to share your thoughts, reader reviews make a meaningful difference for independent authors. Thank you so much.

APPENDIX

The information in this book is drawn from *The Urantia Book*, a 2,097 page book first published in 1955 that claims to be a revelation presented by celestial beings to clarify and expand human understanding of cosmic reality and our place within it. This book about Jesus' early life exclusively cites the 1955 edition which is in the public domain.

You may have never heard of it. Or you may have heard of it and dismissed it. That's fine. What matters is whether the information resonates as true, whether it elevates your understanding, whether it helps you live with greater purpose and confidence.

The Urantia Book has its critics and its devoted students. It's been called everything from the most important spiritual text of the modern era to elaborate fiction. I'm not asking you to accept it blindly. I'm asking you to read it and *then* decide if you think it is true. I do, and I have read it countless times.

The source is less important than the truth it contains. And if you want to explore further, *The Urantia Book* is available online and in print.

The Urantia Book is a comprehensive revelatory tome covering a wide variety of subjects including cosmology, philosophy, history and spirituality. It describes the nature of reality from the perspective of celestial beings and provides detailed information about the structure of the universe, the nature of God, the purpose of human existence, the journey of the soul after death, culminating in the life and teachings of Jesus.

The book is organized into 196 papers grouped into four parts:

Part I: The Central and Superuniverses

Part II: The Local Universe

Part III: The History of Urantia (Earth)

Part IV: The Life and Teachings of Jesus

This book draws exclusively from Part IV.

While I do, at times, exercise creative license, my intention is never to stray from what the book discloses as revelatory fact. Any mistakes are mine to own and correct.

The following references are organized by chapter to help readers locate the source material corresponding to specific content in this book.

NOTES

1. THE ROAD TO BETHLEHEM

1. Paper 122: Birth and Infancy of Jesus, Section 7: The Trip to Bethlehem

2. THE BIRTH OF JOSHUA

1. Paper 122: Birth and Infancy of Jesus, Section 8: The Birth of Jesus

3. THE EARLY YEARS

1. Paper 122: Birth and Infancy of Jesus, Section 9: Presentation in the Temple, Section 10: Birth and Infancy of Jesus, Herod Acts
   Paper 123: The Early Childhood of Jesus, Section 1: Back in Nazareth, Section 2: The Fifth Year (2 B.C.), Section 3: Events of the Sixth Year (1 B.C.), Section 4: The Early Childhood of Jesus, The Seventh Year (A.D. 1), Section 5: The Early Childhood of Jesus, School Days at Nazareth, Section 6: The Early Childhood of Jesus, His Eighth Year (A.D. 2)

4. THE SCHOOL YEARS

1. Paper 124: The Later Childhood of Jesus, Section 1: Jesus' Ninth Year (A.D. 3), Section 2: The Tenth Year (A.D. 4), Section 3: The Eleventh Year (A.D. 5), Section 4: The Twelfth Year (A.D. 6), Section 5: His Thirteenth Year (A.D. 7)

5. THE FIRST PASSOVER

1. Paper 124: The Later Childhood of Jesus, Section 6: The Journey to Jerusalem
   Paper 125: Jesus at Jerusalem, Section 1: Jesus Views the Temple, Section 2: Jesus and the Passover, Section 3: Departure of Joseph and Mary, Section 4: First and Second Days in the Temple, Section 5: The Third Day in the Temple, Section 6: The Fourth Day in the Temple

6. THE DEATH OF JOSEPH

1. Paper 126: The Two Crucial Years, Section 1: His Fourteenth Year, Section 2: The Death of Joseph, Section 3: The Fifteenth Year, Section 4: First Sermon in the Synagogue, Section 5: The Financial Struggle

7. THE ZEALOT CRISIS

1. Paper 127: The Adolescent Years, Section 1: The Sixteenth Year, Section 2: The Seventeenth Year

8. REBECCA

1. Paper 127: The Adolescent Years, Section 3: The Eighteenth Year, Section 4: The Nineteenth Year, Section 5: Rebecca, the Daughter of Ezra, Section 6: His Twentieth Year

9. THE FAMILY YEARS

1. Paper 128: Jesus' Early Manhood, Section 1: The Twenty-First Year, Section 2: The Twenty-Second Year, Section 3: The Twenty-Third Year, Section 4: The Damascus Episode, Section 5: The Twenty-Fourth Year, Section 6: The Twenty-Fifth Year, Section 7: The Twenty-Sixth Year

10. THE BOATBUILDER

1. Paper 129: The Later Adult Life of Jesus, Section 1: The Twenty-Seventh Year, Section 2: The Twenty-Eighth Year, Section 3: The Twenty-Ninth Year, Section 4: The Human Jesus

11. THE DAMASCUS SCRIBE

1. Paper 130: On the Way to Rome, Section 1: At Joppa—Discourse on Jonah, Section 2: At Caesarea

12. ALEXANDRIA

1. Paper 130: On the Way to Rome, Section 3: At Alexandria, Section 4: Discourse on Reality

13. THE ISLAND OF CRETE

1. Paper 130: On the Way to Rome, Section 5: On the Island of Crete, Section 6: The Young Man Who Was Afraid

14. ACROSS THE EMPIRE

1. Paper 130: On the Way to Rome, Section 7: At Carthage—Discourse on Time and Space, Section 8: On the Way to Naples and Rome

15. THE IMPERIAL CITY

1. Paper 132: The Sojourn at Rome, Section 1: True Values, Section 2: Good and Evil, Section 3: Truth and Faith, Section 4: Personal Ministry, Section 5: Counseling the Rich Man

16. THE GREEK WORLD

1. Paper 133: The Return from Rome, Section 1: Mercy and Justice, Section 2: Embarking at Tarentum, Section 3: At Corinth, Section 4: Personal Work in Corinth

17. ATHENS TO CHARAX

1. Paper 133: The Return from Rome, Section 5: At Athens—Discourse on Science, Section 6: At Ephesus—Discourse on the Soul, Section 7: The Sojourn at Cyprus—Discourse on Mind, Section 8: At Antioch, Section 9: In Mesopotamia

18. MOUNT HERMON

1. Paper 134: The Transition Years, Section 1: The Thirtieth Year, Section 2: The Caravan Trip to the Caspian, Section 3: The Urmia Lectures, Section 4: Sovereignty—Divine and Human, Section 5: Political Sovereignty, Section 6: Law, Liberty, and Sovereignty, Section 7: The Thirty-First Year, Section 8: The Sojourn on Mount Hermon, Section 9: The Time of Waiting

19. THE VOICE IN THE WILDERNESS

1. Paper 135: John the Baptist, Section 1: John Becomes a Nazarite, Section 2: The Death of Zacharias, Section 3: The Life of a Shepherd, Section 4: The Death of Elizabeth, Section 5: The Kingdom of God, Section 6: John Begins to Preach, Section 7: John Journeys North, Section 8: Meeting of Jesus and John, Section 9: Forty Days of Preaching; Paper 136: Baptism and the Forty Days, Section 1: Concepts of the Expected Messiah, Section 2: The Baptism of Jesus

20. THE GREAT DECISIONS

1. Paper 136: Baptism and the Forty Days, Section 3: The Forty Days, Section 4: Plans for Public Work, Section 5: The First Great Decision, Section 6: The Second Decision, Section 7: The Third Decision, Section 8: The Fourth Decision, Section 9: The Fifth Decision, Section 10: The Sixth Decision

ABOUT THE AUTHOR

Michael Vincent has spent over twenty years studying the life of Jesus through sources beyond the traditional Gospels. His work focuses on making profound spiritual teachings accessible to modern readers—people hungry for substance, not platitudes.

He believes the real Jesus is far more compelling than the sanitized figure of religious art: more human, more approachable, and yet more extraordinary than most people imagine.

The *Universe Maker from Nazareth* saga represents his attempt to tell that story in full.

michaelvincentauthor.com

instagram.com/michaelvincent_author
tiktok.com/@michael.vincent.author
youtube.com/@MichaelVincent-Author
amazon.com/author/havona-press

ALSO BY MICHAEL VINCENT

Where We Go When We Die: Life After Death Across the Universe

Fusion with God: The Path to Immortality

The Angelic Orders: Cosmic Servants of the Infinite

Upcoming Books:

The Public Ministry: The Real Story of Jesus Beyond the Gospels (The *Universe Maker from Nazareth* series, Book Two)

The Final Week: The Real Story of Jesus Beyond the Gospels (The *Universe Maker from Nazareth* series, Book Three)

The Nine Races: The Forgotten Origin of Humanity

Before Humans: The Drama of World-Making

Marcus Aurelius, Rodan of Alexandria, and Jesus of Nazareth: A Philosopher's Journey